MAKING WAVES
The Politics of Communications

Radical Science 16
Edited by the Radical Science Collective

*'... an association in which the free development of each
is the condition of the free development of all'*

Free Association Books / London / 1985

302.234
MAK

Making Waves
Radical Science 16

Published January 1985 by
Free Association Books
26 Freegrove Road, London N7

British Library Cataloguing in Publication Data
Making Waves.
  (Radical Science. ISSN 0305-0963; no. 16)
  1. Communication – Social aspects
  I. Radical Science Collective   III. Series
  302.2   HM258

  ISBN 0-946960-16-X

4.1.89

Contents

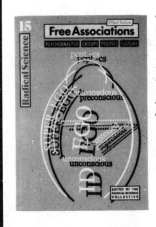

The editors of Radical Science gratefully acknowledge permission to reprint the diagram on the cover of **Radical Science 15** from Sigmund Freud, *New Introductory Lectures on Psychoanalysis*, published by the Hogarth Press and Institute of Psychoanalysis in Great Britain and by W.W. Norton & Co in the USA.

MAKING WAVES

The traditional warning, 'Don't make waves', has become obsolete. Today we are invited to make lots of waves, to communicate more than ever before, in ways that are supposed to lighten our work and enhance our leisure. New technologies, we are told, will give us unprecedented freedom of choice in the messages we receive and even send. With our home computer we can write letters and essays in immaculate form; with cable we can take part in opinion polls. With the two combined we will be able to shop from home and even work from home: freedom from unnecessary travel. And satellites can connect us to anyone in the world: a global village reducing the distance between people.

So we are all reassured. Nightmare visions of George Orwell's *1984* have surely proven unfounded. There is no Big Brother imposing propaganda and surveillance on us from enormous screens. Rather, we voluntarily wire ourselves up – on a small, friendly scale – to enjoy the benefits on offer. Indeed, in this 'post-industrial' society, based on information rather than industrial production, we reach the pinnacle of human freedom, or at least so we are told.

But what kind of waves will be made in this electronic paradise? Are we offered simply ...

– the freedom to convert knowledge into 'data', into information?
– the freedom to reduce out lives even further to buying and selling?
– the freedom to make our leisure time as programmed as our working time, to privatise leisure?
– the freedom to let agencies collect even more information about us?

We may well ask: Will 'communications' mean prosthetic substitutes for real human contact? Will making waves mean more commoditisation and policing of daily life? Or might oppositional designs and uses be possible? Towards answering these questions, the essays here explore both the oppressive and liberatory possibilities of communications technologies.
¶   Hi-tech homeworking has arrived, as home computers have become a direct instrument of wage-labour for women who can't easily get away from home responsibilities to attend office jobs.

Ursula Huws shows that, far from being a great opportunity for women, this trend provides an opportunity for employers to isolate, cheapen and control their workers. So far this 'terminal isolation' has affected mainly the higher-paid computer workers; could it extend to clerical workers as a whole?

¶   Infotech has barely touched most of the Third World, even in terms of importation, much less indigenous production. Armand Mattelart argues, however, that the main problem is not Third World access to infotech, since its small presence there is geared largely to 'state security' and multinationals' control over both

Dan Thibidoux

culture and production. Infotech should be seen as no less part of the problem than earlier technologies used for exploiting the Third World.

¶ What would it be like to design and install an 'electronic bulletin board'? Such a noble aim led the Community Memory collective through a very long detour: setting up a commercial software firm to raise the money. Here Tom Athanasiuo describes the contradictions that inevitably arose, in his case study of high-tech alternativism', operating in the heart of alternative America: Berkeley, California.

¶ Expansion of the radio airwaves – either through licensing or extra-legal pirates – has met conflicting responses from the media left in Britain. Fearing that such expansion would necessarily benefit commercial interests, some have supported stricter state regulation. Here Richard Barbrook argues for community radio as an alternative to both state and commercial control, by directly involving oppositional groups in making the radio programmes; no mere pipedream, his proposal has been assured funding from the Greater London Council.

¶ As for television, some on the left condemn it as irremediably an instrument of capitalist domination. Doug Kellner offers a counter-example from his own experience of broadcasting *Alternative Views*, a cable tv series in the USA. He describes how a small, dedicated group was able to use a (otherwise nominal) 'public access' clause in the cable licence to get airtime, resulting in a unique experience of genuine radical tv in one of America's richest university and hi-tech towns: Austin, Texas.

¶ Has Nicaragua's television been revolutionised? Although it remains influenced by US models of professionalism, tv there has allowed some space for innovation – especially video – providing news, entertainment and education. Here Dee Dee Halleck gives a first-hand account of how Nicaragua makes 'live-from-the-revolution' video.

¶ According to the full-page ads we often see for telecoms systems as human progress, the newest technologies seem to have developed almost by natural evolution from ancient smoke signals and hieroglyphics. According to Michael Chanan's rebuttal here, using the example of Reuters' telegraph and its successors, these systems did not simply 'grow'; rather, they were designed specially for transmitting financial and military information. Furthermore, when Reuters did come to compete as a commercial news service, it produced a homogenised journalistic language that still dominates the 'quality press' today.

¶ 'E.T.', one of the all-time biggest money-spinners, is commonly seen as a children's film. Yet it has held a peculiar fascination and emotional appeal for men, many of whom have gone back to see it several times. To help explain this response, Dave Albury describes its 'male fantasy of power', linking masculinity and technology in a different way from most science-fiction films.

photo: Annie Silverleaf

The Future of Family Life?

TERMINAL ISOLATION
The Atomisation of Work and Leisure in the Wired Society

Ursula Huws

The home is a subject which has received little serious attention in recent socialist thought. Implicit in most arguments is a notion that the home is a space somewhat apart from the mainstream of economic activity, with internal social relations which are relatively autonomous and an economic role which can be simply and straightforwardly encapsulated in the single word 'consumption'.

Where this notion has been challenged, it has generally been by feminists, who have demonstrated the importance of the home as the site of the reproduction of labour power and the formation of gender relations. They have insisted that it is only in relation to the 'private' social relations of the home that it is possible to understand many features of the 'public' world, such as the occupational segregation of women in the workplace and the role of male violence in enforcing female compliance with a patriarchal order. Such theorising, most of which has been directed towards developing an understanding of patriarchy in the totality of its relationship with capitalism, has inevitably concentrated on those aspects of home life which appear to be most universal; the theorising has lacked historical specificity. Thus many of the changes which have taken place in the relationship between the home and the rest of the economy, and in its internal structure, have passed almost unrecorded. Without an understanding of these changes, it is difficult to grasp the impact of information technology on home life.

It is the purpose of this article to examine some of these developments, to look at the growing importance of the home as the locus of profound shifts in the boundaries between what is 'public' and what is 'private', and to examine some of the effects of information technology on the home. Without a clear analysis of the home, and political strategies based on such an analysis, socialist policies are doomed to failure. Needless to say, an article like this cannot provide such an analysis; it can merely sketch in some of the features which it would incorporate. If it makes a contribution towards opening up a debate among socialists on the role of the home, it will have served its purpose well. Before examining the effects of information technology on home life and their political implications, I should like to outline some of the other changes which have been taking place in the home, which set the context for the present upheaval and those predicted for the future.

Political Economy of the Home

Perhaps the most obvious and best documented of these changes has been the huge growth in owner occupation, given an added impetus in Britain by Government policies. It was recognised at the beginning of the century – by the philanthropist and capitalist Andrew Carnegie, among others – that a working class which owned its own housing was the best possible protection against strikes and uprisings.[1] But such changes in political attitudes are not the only result of home ownership. Besides creating a vested interest in the status quo, greater dependence on a regular source of income and a habit of hoarding, home ownership also has the effect of reducing mobility for whole households and for individuals within them. The mortgage can often be a more effective bond than a marriage licence in cementing people to each other and to particular locations. As the supply of rented accommodation deteriorates in both quality and quantity, owner occupation increasingly becomes a compulsory requirement for those seeking reasonable security and value for money.

Parallel with this compulsory investment in bricks and mortar goes another requirement, the result of major changes in the structure of industry outside the home. This is the necessity to invest in a whole range of capital goods, from cars to washing machines. These goods can be seen as the results of the process whereby service industries have been progressively commoditised. This process has been chronicled by Jonathan Gershuny,[2] who has shown how over the past three decades private forms of transport have been substituted for public ones, washing machines have ousted laundry services and the purchase of television sets has replaced visits to the cinema or live entertainment. As these new commodities have spread, use of the older services which they replace has become relatively expensive, and they have tended to disappear. We have thus increasingly been left with the choice of buying or doing without. The working class could, in fact, be said to be required to invest in its own means of reproduction to an ever greater extent.

The substitution of the purchase of commodities for the hire of services also has the effect of substituting the unpaid labour of the consumer for the paid work of the service worker, and creating a number of new tasks connected with the purchase, operation and upkeep of these domestic appliances. Other aspects of the rationalisation and automation of services also produce new types of unpaid work which the consumer must carry out, in the form of self service. Where services have traditionally involved labour-intensive interaction with the public by service workers, this has become the norm in recent years in a range of industries including retailing, catering, banking, transport (petrol sales; ticket dispensing) and various comparatively new forms of information retrieval. In the guise of 'do-it-yourself', self service has also replaced traditional crafts, such as cabinet-making, and trades like painting and decorating, while giving rise to the growth of profitable new industries manufacturing the tools and products which make such deskilling possible.

Again, it is comparative cost advantage which has pushed consumers into choosing these self-service forms over their traditional counterparts based on the waged labour of large numbers of service workers or tradespeople. The older forms have in most cases come to appear anachronistic – either luxuries for the rich, or inefficient and wasteful methods reserved for those without the ability or wit to service themselves. In many cases, of course, the traditional forms were never within the reach of large portions of the working class, and the rise of self service is perceived as raising their standard of living, bringing new comforts and status symbols within their grasp.

We can see that these processes have together resulted in a radical change in the job description of the consumer, or 'consumption worker', as s/he has been more accurately designated by some commentators.[3] As some traditional tasks have been automated and deskilled, numerous new ones have been added, many of them formerly the province of paid service workers ranging from delivery boys to laundresses, from bank tellers to plasterers. These tasks are carried out singly and in isolation. They generally involve the use of technology or chemical substances whose workings and effects are not understood by their users. Housewives are then placed entirely in the hands of the 'experts' when it comes to utilising them. The labour process is thus increasingly controlled by the designers and manufacturers of these commodities, by means of fine-printed instructions which are disobeyed at the user's peril, with standards set by advertisements, and by less overt ideological pressures.[4]

As consumption work becomes more private, and more and more of the energies of consumption workers are directed towards the improvement, maintenance and protection of their individual homes and possessions, there is an accompanying erosion of public, collective forms of service. The pub, the cinema, the football stadium, the political meeting room; all have seen a spectacular drop in attendance over the past few decades. So too have a huge range of small businesses such as cafes, corner grocers' shops and high-street ironmongers, ousted by giant chains of fast-food outlets, supermarkets and do-it-yourself shops which rely on self service to keep their costs low. As workplaces, they have changed spectacularly, increasingly providing only employment which is casual, deskilled and machine-paced, closer to factory work than to the old-fashioned service work which was characterised by a more leisurely pace, specialised skills and a high degree of personal interaction with customers. From the customer's point of view, the changes are perhaps even more far-reaching, for these places represent the only spaces (outside their own workplaces if they are fortunate enough to be employed in a collective space) where they can come together to exchange news and views, and develop an alternative interpretation of their daily experience from that handed down by the media. As any community activist will testify, encounters in public laundries, local shopping precincts, pubs and the like have been crucial to the development of campaigns such as those to improve housing or oppose dangerous traffic schemes. At the more general level of the formation of political attitudes, it seems likely that they are also important. The General Election of 1983 was widely experienced as the first almost exclusively 'media election' in the UK, and it can be conjectured that the decline of public meetings, both formal and informal, played a part in Labour's crushing defeat. As public space is eroded and replaced by privatised activity, there is a corresponding loss of such alternative culture.

So far, I have discussed the changes taking place within the home as though they are gender-neutral in their effects. This is, of course, far from being the case. Most consumption work is done by women, who are disproportionately affected by these changes.

Where traditional domestic skills are disappearing, they are generally women's skills, but the skills involved in designing and repairing the new household technologies tend to be held fairly exclusively by men. Thus the new technologies can be seen, not as liberating women, but as providing another means whereby male power over women's domestic labour is reinforced, analogous to the control over women's bodies which medical technology has given to a largely male medical profession. Women too are the main sufferers from the increased volume of domestic labour and its redefinition to include new consumption-related tasks.[5]

Finally, we must note the effects on women of the erosion of public space. This,has several dimensions: Firstly, most women are considerably poorer than men, either completely economically dependent on them or subsisting independently on wages which are much lower. They are thus much less likely to be able to afford to purchase private alternatives to inadequate public services, such as cars, telephones or video recorders; hence they are more severely incapacitated by the loss of community facilities. Secondly, women are the main carers, more likely to be tied to the home and neighbourhood all day by the need to care for young children, or aged or handicapped dependants. Thirdly, women and children are most vulnerable to the increasing physical dangers present in the environment. Today, many children must play indoors for fear of traffic, just as their mothers and older sisters are confined to the house at night by the threat of rape. The absence of safe collective space, policed by the presence of neighbours, keeps many virtually imprisoned in the isolation of their homes.

Structure of Employment

To understand the full force of the effects information technology will have on women's lives in the home, it is also necessary to take a more general look at the changes which have been taking place in relation to women's position elsewhere in the economy.

The postwar period has witnessed a large and unprecedented influx of women into the labour market. In particular, women, many of them working part-time, were the majority of those who flooded into the expanding service industries, so that by 1980 they formed over 40% of all workers in employment, with over a third involved in clerical work of some description.[6] During this period there has been a decline in the family wage, and most households are now dependent on female earnings to maintain themselves above the poverty line. Women too have come to expect to earn an independent income during most of their adult lives.

However, since the mid-70s the concept of a woman's right to work has come under attack from several quarters. Cutbacks in public expenditure have removed many of the facilities, such as nurseries and day-centres for the elderly and handicapped, which enable carers to go out to work. Changes in employment protection legislation have taken away many rights, particularly for part-time workers and those employed by small firms, in relation to maternity and protection against unfair dismissal. In addition, for the first time since the 50s, there has been an ideological onslaught on working mothers. Revamped theories of maternal deprivation and the doctrine of 'community care' have meshed with the more traditional notion that male unemploy-ment can be solved by women's return to the home, to produce a climate of opinion in which it is increasingly difficult for women to fight for their jobs.[7]

And it has been during the same decade that women's jobs themselves have been increasingly under threat, partly as a result of the public spending cuts which have placed many service jobs in schools and hospitals at risk; partly through the general effects of the recession and the international restructuring of industries like electronics, textiles and clothing which have traditionally been major employers of women; and partly through the effects of information technology which is being introduced into precisely those areas where most women work – shops, banks and offices. Already this technology has radically transformed skill require-ments in these industries, and introduced machine-pacing and a number of new health hazards associated with continuous screen-watching and stress.[8] It has also brought about some job loss, though so far not on the scale predicted in the late 70s when many commentators forecast that over a third of information-processing jobs would disappear as a result of new technology.

The reason for this is not, in my view, that these forecasters were wrong. Rather, we have so far witnessed only the first stage of what is essentially a two-stage introduction of information technology. In the first stage, the key technology is that of microelectronics, with its capacity to cheapen and miniaturise, so that computing power can be widely introduced into information-processing functions which have previously been executed manually, perhaps with mechanical assistance. This stage is already well underway and has resulted in a proliferation of small, disparate computing systems: here a word processor, there a microcomputer, there again a computerised control system. It is rare for these systems to be interconnected, and most information still passes from paper, into electronic form, and back into paper again during its useful life.

Stage two of the introduction of information technology depends much more heavily on telecommunications technology; it largely consists of connecting all these separate systems up to each other. It is only when this has occurred on a wide scale that the major productivity increases will take place, since it is only at this stage that the labour-intensive paper processing phase of information handling can be eliminated. Already there in embryonic form in many industries, it is this telecommunications-based wave of technological change which is about to break over us.

Transfer of Work to the Home

The effect of the new, cheap telecommunications data links will not just be to cause redundancies; it will also bring about fundamental changes in the location of information processing work. With cheap methods of transmitting digital information, whether by cable or satellite, distance ceases to be an important factor in the location of terminals in relation to their parent computers. Information can be input or retrieved wherever it is convenient to site the terminal and its operator. This could be a distant office or the worker's own home. It is this fact, more than any other, which underlies the often-repeated statement that information technology is 'good for the family'. It is seen, quite simply, as providing the means whereby women workers can be returned to the home, and to the dominion of their husbands, without the loss of their services as a cheap form of clerical labour.[9]

Consider the scenario: there are in Britain upwards of three million women clerical workers, of whom many have children and many have been trained to work with VDUs and keyboards. While increasing numbers are being expelled from their jobs, few have access to alternatives, or to facilities which would enable them to seek them. Yet their need for an independent income has never been greater, because of rising male unemployment and cutbacks in social security benefit levels. From the employers' point of view, there is a need to cut costs and a strong trend towards casualising the workforce wherever possible.[10] The employment of home-workers saves on overheads such as city-centre floor-space, sick pay, holiday pay and pension schemes. It is also an effective means of preventing unionisation and keeping wage levels as low as possible. The increasing home-centredness of most people's lives, and the deterioration of public transport and childcare facilities, give an added incentive to such developments, with the final shove a psychological one, coming from the increasing hostility directed at women who go out to work and abandon their children.

These factors underlie the numerous forecasts of massive increases in homeworking by the 1990s.[11] In purely physical terms, the ground seems well prepared for an increase in new technology-related homeworking in Britain. We have the highest per capita ownership of personal computers in the world; a population

---

PLANNING FOR HOMEWORK

Invitation to a Conference

The Trustees of H.A.C.T. are pleased to extend this Invitation for you to attend, as their Guest, the one-day Conference they are convening at the headquarters of the Royal Institute of British Architects, Portland Place, London in May.

The Conference is restricted and 400 Invitations only are being issued with due discretion to those within Whitehall, Local Authorities, Industry, Commerce, designated Professions, Academia, Building Industry/Housing Finance and the Press. This is to the end that those assembled should give serious consideration now to making the revision of the design requirements of existing and future housing stock a major priority.

Specifically the Trust regards it as assured and predictable that the future patterns of work, employment and leisure will demand housing which is not merely attuned to future dynamic living patterns but facilitates a wider range of home-based activity; whether that be gainful or an expressive release of energy, feeling and ambition.

Today, most people recognise from any vantage point that economic changes centred around the cost of labour prevailing in Western economies, and the predictable advance of technology, are transforming established patterns of work and the matching rewards. The Trustees merely echo those perceptions when they assert that Industry and Commerce will not, and could not as some dimension of social responsibility, again 'carry' unskilled labour in the factories and commercial centres of tomorrow.

With 10 million Pensioners, a benchmark of 3 million unemployed and a dynamic recycling of skilled labour which necessitates the retraining and education of large cadres of youth, it seems clear on such

largely concentrated in dense easy-to-cable clusters in the metropolitan county areas; a Government which has rushed through plans to cable the country on terms extremely advantageous to private industry with indecent haste, and is now trying to sell off the national telecommunications grid at a knockdown price. Britain is a world leader in the viewdata technology which provides one way that such remote working can be carried out; one UK company, Rediffusion Computers, is already manufacturing 'teleputer' workstations for precisely this purpose.

Yet all is not progressing quite as this outline might suggest.

---

grounds alone that many households will spend far more time at home than hitherto.

Already research has established that many large companies plan to have a significant part of their Staff working from home. The Trustees refute the current insular assumptions, voiced by wiseacres and some Developers, that those who will consequently seek the flexibility (and job mobility) of modern home-working facilities will readily procure the means for the desired priority changes in their housing when events press.

In summary so far then. The Trustees believe poor housing formerly identified as being defective for structural reasons, and more recently as socially divisive for planning blunders, could acquire a new ruinous dimension by the end of the century. For without design changes it will prejudice low income householders by denying them the means to engage in certain activities for gain or severely limit the social cohesion of a family that might otherwise generate more unity through the vicarious bonds of greater activity at home.

The Trustees are the first to realise that they are ill-placed to advocate these revisions and, in the context of the Private and Public housing programmes, demand priority changes in the U.K. long term economy.

However, it follows that, if detailed evidence and general arguments are there for those of goodwill and authority to aggregate, then there should be sufficient support from, and opinion within, Industry and Commerce to proclaim these as new prerequisite factors of productivity warranting the redesign of housing. Later, this could be augmented with what is, for many, the more arcane hypothesis of the social benefits of revived family unity and the re-emergence of the 'headship' factor . . .

John Willis DFM ACIS
Vice Chairman
Housing Associations
Charitable Trust

Investment in cable has not been as readily forthcoming as was anticipated. Mercury, the private telecommunications company set up to compete with British Telecom, is in deep financial trouble, with no prospect of any worthwhile return for its investors for a decade. Many of the companies which put in bids for local cable franchises in 1983 seem to have got off to a bungling start, unable to put together packages which appeal to their potential advertisers.

This suggests that a nationwide high-capacity interactive electronic grid, of a cheapness to make it cost-effective for use as a substitute for transporting low-paid workers in and out of city-centre sites, is a little further off than some of the more the enthusiastic commentators have forecast; it will probably not be a reality until well into the 90s. The days of mass telecommuting are not yet with us. Ironically enough, a centralised state telecommunications authority committed to such investment would probably have succeeded in bringing it about much more quickly. However, this is no reason for complacency. The British Telecom grid is already being used to export some types of office work into the home and to develop other forms of interactive service. And satellite technology also has the potential for relocating information processing work; indeed, it is already being used internationally for that purpose.

Because of the relatively high cost and low capacity of the telephone network, it is currently mainly used in the UK for professional grade work in fields in which there is a comparative skills shortage. In a survey of new-technology homeworking I carried out for the Equal Opportunities Commission in 1982, nine out of ten of the sample were computer professionals – programmers, systems analysts or technical authors (specialist writers of computer manuals, who are generally ex-programmers). Typically, they were women in their mid-thirties with children under five. Their earnings, averaging between £4 and £5 per hour, were high compared with those of traditional-type homeworkers stuffing teddy bears or sewing buttons, but significantly lower than going rates in the industry for similar office-based work. Most suffered from isolation and gave the impression that, were it not for their childcare responsibilities, they would both prefer to be working in an office and be better off in terms of wage-levels and seniority if they were not based at home.

All the signs are that homeworking of this type is on the increase and beginning to extend to other types of work involving the extensive use of computers, such as various middle management functions. Moving further down the office hierarchy we also find homeworking, much of it an extension of the casual typing and envelope-stuffing which has been done at home for decades. New technology is beginning to make its presence felt here too, in the form of home-based word-processing, but so far it is rare to find this linked on-line to an office computer. This is unlikely to happen until telecommunications costs are cheaper.[12]

Meanwhile, interactive services are creeping into British homes under different guises. After a number of false starts, the BT Prestel viewdata system is making some headway, although a high proportion of its users are businesses. One scheme based on it is the Nottingham Building Society's 'Homelink' service, which combines the Prestel information service with a home banking service. As an incentive to potential users, the hardware is available free to those with an investment of over £1,000 in the Building Society or a mortgage with the company, but some usage charges are still made, mainly to cover the comparatively expensive element of telephone time. A limited home shopping experiment has been set up in the London area for homelink subscribers, but this still seems to have progressed little further than an amusing toy for the middle classes, which is also the status of similar, larger-scale experiments in the United States, such as QUBE.

It is sobering to remember in this context how rapidly other products, such as video recorders, have progressed from this status to becoming an accepted part of the equipment of working class homes. Nevertheless, it seems likely that the high cost of telephone connection, and the labour-intensive nature of the delivery services which must accompany home-based shopping, will be real brakes on the progress of this development. One home shopping experiment in Gateshead relies on subsidies from the local authority and the Manpower Services Commission to sustain its ordering and delivery services.

Another factor which seems likely to hamper the progress of home-based interactive services stems from the very fact of the male domination of the design of the systems. In one Japanese experiment, in Higashi-Ikoma, a large number of services were made available for an experimental period between 2 pm and 6 pm on weekdays, and hence to a largely female, housebound audience. The system allowed for limited two-way communication, including the use of a video camera, so that users could transmit pictures of themselves or their children to other participants in the experiment. From the point of view of those who set up the experiment, it was a failure. There seemed to be little interest in using the information services provided, and a great reluctance to use any service which cost money (in line with the British experience of Prestel). What the system was used for, with enthusiasm, was to make friends. Having seen pictures of neighbours and their children on the TV screen, women felt able to approach them in the supermarket and strike up an acquaintance. They were using the technology as a means to break down isolation and attempt to get out of their homes, rather than to stay in them, as the designers appear to have intended. The ability to do this was, of course, a direct result of the smallness of the experiment. The larger the number of people involved, the lower would be the chances of meeting someone seen on the screen.[13] The results of this experiment give heartening evidence that many women will resist the introduction of systems which so clearly fail to address their needs, if these systems are offered simply as entertainment or aids to home management. It seems likely in the long term, however, that other criteria will take over. The systems, like the present generation of home computers, will be purchased as toys for the male members of the household, aids to the children's education, or prerequisites for earning a living.

The other factor which complicates the simple scenario of work being transferred directly from offices into homes is the existence of satellite technology which makes it just as easy to transport office work to other countries. Routine work, such as data entry, is already being shipped offshore by a number of US-based companies, where wages are a quarter of those of American clerical staff. Sites chosen for this intensive, low-skill work are usually ex-British colonies in the Third World, such as India and the West Indies, where English is spoken; but at least one company uses women in Ireland for long-distance office work. It seems likely that a situation will develop in office work very like that in traditional manufacturing industries relying on cheap female labour, such as the garment industry, where two workforces – homeworkers in the Developed countries and Third World workers based in sweatshops – are played off against each other by the employers.[14]

Implications for Home Life

Whatever the exact timescale of these developments, and the global breakdown of the division of office labour which results, it seems clear that the trend is overwhelmingly in the direction of casualisation and the reconstitution of the home as a workspace. Taken together with the trends outlined at the beginning of this article, this represents a massive transfer of costs by capital onto workers, who now must bear not only many of the costs of what might be called the means of reproduction but also those of the means of production.

Workers are now expected to bear the costs of house purchase and maintenance and interest charges on them; the cost of a range of capital goods to carry out the new domestic tasks which replace service industries (washing machines, electric drills, video recorders, etc.); much of the transport and storage costs of consumable products (trips to supermarkets, energy to run home freezers, etc.); the assembly costs of many consumer durables (self-assemble furniture, toys, etc.); the cost of a good deal of service labour (bank tellers, petrol pump attendants, shop assistants, etc.); the cost of some capital equipment necessary for paid work (industrial sewing machines, home computers, typewriters, etc.); and, increasingly, a wide range of overheads normally provided by employers – such as heating, energy, canteen, and floorspace costs, and the costs of benefits such as paid holidays, sickness pay, maternity benefits, redundancy pay and pensions – which most homeworkers are denied.

A superficial perusal of this list might suggest that such a development is progressive. Surely, one might argue, if workers now *own* all these things, then that gives them greater control over their living and working lives. In fact, of course, nothing could be further from the truth. All these developments are accompanied by a loss of control and a tightening of the leash by which these workers are attached to capital.

This control is exercised in several ways. Firstly, it is strengthened by the atomisation of the workforce. Isolated in their individual homes, it is increasingly difficult for them to combine to defend their interests, whether these are as consumption workers or as employees (or, indeed, in any other capacity – as women, as blacks, as disabled people, as parents or whatever). Secondly, in relation to new technology homeworkers, control is designed into the very form of the machines and systems used. It is now a standard component of any software package used for data entry, for instance, that it closely monitors the performance of its operator, by counting the number of keystrokes per minute, the error rate, the number of items dealt with, the length and frequency of breaks, or any other variable useful to the employer. This is used to police the workers quite as effectively as many more traditional methods of supervision. Some companies have brought such remote control to a fine art, even exploiting the solidarity among workers in the drive to boost productivity. One French hire purchase company operates a scheme whereby workers are monitored both as individuals and as work groups. Only the latter records are made available to the women who operate the VDU terminals processing loan repayments. The ·group which performs best over a period of time is rewarded by being given what is regarded as more pleasant work to do for a time – chasing up defaulting debtors over the telephone. Loyalty to other group members is the main mechanism which prevents slackening the work pace.[15]

Even more sinister (if less direct) in its implications, is a third form of control by individuals which information technology makes continually easier. This is the control which can be exercised through surveillance. The more functions are carried out from computer terminals, the more records of such transactions can be stored in easily accessible digital form. Already a bewilderingly wide range of records of individuals are kept by a variety of state and commercial agencies. Teleworking, teleshopping and telebanking will add immeasurably to these, enabling more and more sophisticated portraits of individuals and their activities and predelictions to be built up. In the US, home shopping experiments are already being used to build 'consumer profiles' of individual users, to enable advertising to be precisely targeted. Such data could as easily be used by the state to identify potential subversives or those involved in oppositional activities.

Big Brother, it seems, arrived right on schedule in 1984.

Conclusions

What conclusions can be drawn from these tendencies?

● Firstly, it can be seen that workers are being dragged ever more firmly into dependence on a wage in order to support the investment which is now required in the fabric of their homes and the technology with which they must fill them. Lack of a wage creates increasing relative deprivation.

● Secondly, there is a growing atomisation of the working class, with an erosion of collective public space and of means of organising and communicating. This strengthens centralised ideological control.

● Thirdly, women, far from being liberated by technology – domestic or otherwise – are thereby being placed into positions of greater dependence on men.

● Fourthly, despite a massive transfer of labour costs from service industries onto consumers and the growth of new forms of consumption work, a loss of control over the labour process of consumption work is taking place.This closely parallels the loss of control over labour processes in the workplace which automation brings.

● Fifthly, women seem likely to continue forming an ever-larger proportion of the paid workforce, but this role is increasingly likely to be carried out in the isolation of the home.

What are the implications of these developments for socialists and feminists? Perhaps the most important questions which arise are those relating to control: control of the design of technology and systems; control of the work process, be it paid or unpaid work; control of information; and control of the means of communication.

Control is an issue which has figured prominently in many recent debates on the left (several of which have featured in past issues of the Radical Science series). The experience of nationalised industries in Britain, for instance, has demonstrated that public ownership does not constitute public accountability or control. Women have learned that the existence of medical technology and drugs with the apparent potential for improving health has not given them more control over their own bodies but has, on the contrary, handed more power to the male-dominated medical profession. Similarly, workers' struggles over health and safety have taught the crucial importance of control over the pace of work in minimising hazards. The spread of information technology raises similar questions; it gives an added urgency to the search for organisational forms and demands which will enable people to wrest back some of the control over their daily lives which is increasingly being taken from them and placed in the power of the centralised institutions of capital and the state. Some existing activities point in this direction – popular planning policies like those of the Greater London Council, workers' struggles against casualisation and for health and safety in the workplace, experiments in collectivising domestic services, campaigns against cutbacks in public services. However, it appears that few socialist programmes address these questions in any systematic, large-scale way. In order to do so effectively, they must be rooted in a clear analysis of the effects of technological, social and economic change – not just at the level of the state, region or town, or of particular industries, but at the level of the individual home. It is in the home that Big Brother's power is most felt, in the helplessness that the single isolated woman or man feels when interfacing with his systems. Only when these mechanisms are fully understood can his power be combatted.

Notes

1. Quoted in Barbara Ehrenreich and Deirdre English, *For Her Own Good*, Pluto Press, 1979. Ehrenreich and English also provide an enlightening discussion of the implications of this trend.

2. Jonathan Gershuny, *After Industrial Society? The Emerging Self-Service Economy*, Macmillan, 1978.

3. This is the term used by Batya Weinbaum and Amy Bridges in their landmark article, 'The Other Side of the Paycheck', in *Monthly Review* July/August 1976 (reprinted two years later in the Monthly Review Press anthology, *Capitalist Patriarchy and the Case for Socialist Feminism*). It is a term which accurately describes much of the unpaid activity which all women and some men have to engage in, without confining it exclusively to the home, as is done implicitly by the term 'housework'.

4. I have described this process in greater detail in an article entitled 'Domestic Technology: Liberator or Enslaver?', in *Scarlet Women* 14, (January 1982).

5. The proliferation of domestic appliances in the home appears to have been directly paralleled by a rise in the number of hours devoted to housework by housewives in homes without domestic servants. According to surveys analysed by Ann Oakley in *Housewife*, Penguin, 1974, weekly hours of housework increased from an average of 62 in 1929 to 77 in 1971.

6. *New Earnings Surveys*, Department of Employment, 1980-83.

7. The tone was set for the incoming Conservative Government in Britain in June 1979 by Lord Spens, opening a debate on unemployment in the House of Lords. He said, 'If women could be persuaded to stay at home – especially those with children – that would provide a solution.' He added, 'I am not saying that they should not be occupied – just that they should not compete in the market for paid jobs.'

8. For a more detailed discussion of the effects of new technology on women's employment, see Ursula Huws, *Your Job in the Eighties*, Pluto Press, 1982.

9. The connection between the subservient role of women in the family and the growth of homeworking is made quite explicitly in many of the public statements about new technology. Both the Prime Minister, Margaret Thatcher, and the ex-Minister for Information Technology, Kenneth Baker, for instance, said that cable networks would be 'good for the family' when announcing the British Government's blueprint for cable networks, the 1983 White Paper on Cable. A conference held in May 1984, organised by the Housing Associations Charitable Trust and addressed by planners and industrialists, entitled 'Planning for Homework' went even further. The invitation to it enthused, among other things, about the way that homeworking would 'restore the headship factor' to families. See the excerpts reprinted here, both for the illustration of this point and the delights of its prose style.

10. The casualisation of the labour force, encouraged by the repeal of some Employment Protection legislation, has been proceeding apace in Europe, the United States and Japan. Some statistical evidence of this

trend in the UK was published in the *Employment Gazette* in July 1982 in an article entitled 'Recent Developments in Working Patterns'. More recently it has been the subject of some comment in the business press. See for instance 'Flexible Firm Takes Shape' in the financial pages of the *Guardian*, 18 April 1984.

11. Prophecies of a large-scale shift of work to the home using telecommunications links began to be made in the wake of the energy crisis of the early 70s. It was predicted by Baran and Lipinski, in a report, *The Future of the Telephone Industry*, published in 1971 by the Californian Institute for the Future, that all US executives would be homeworkers by 1990. A Japanese study carried out two years later for the Nippon Telephone and Telegraph Public Corporation forecast that 65% of white-collar workers would be home-based. After excluding clerical-type occupations, another Californian study (D.W. Jones, *Must We Travel? The Potential of Communication as a Substitute for Urban Travel*, Stanford University, 1973) estimated that 22% of the total number of journeys to work could be eliminated by homeworking. In Britain, British Telecom carried out a study which concluded that some 13½ million workers, from 24 separate occupational groups, were potential candidates for being shifted to the home (Joan Glover, *Long-Range Social Forecasts: Working From Home*, British Telecom, 1974). As the reality approaches, forecasters have become more cautious about making quantitative predictions. However, the association of new technology and homeworking has already been made in the public mind. It is now a commonplace – of the rhetoric of pop futurologists, politicians and media pundits – not only that new technology will 'enable us all to work from the comfort of our living rooms' but also that this is unquestionably a Good Thing.

12. See my account of this project, which includes a general discussion of recent developments in new technology-related homeworking as well as an analysis of the UK survey of high-tech homeworkers: Ursula Huws, *The New Homeworkers*, Low Pay Unit, 1984.

13. This experiment is described in detail by Tarja Cronberg and Inga-Lise Sangregorio under the title, 'More of the Same: The Impact of Information Technology on Domestic Life in Japan', in *Development Dialogue* 1981: 2.

14. This development is explored in greater depth in Ursula Huws, 'The Runaway Office Jobs', *International Labour Reports* No. 2, 1984.

15. Described by Richard Clavaud in 'Le Teletravail', *Telesoft* No.1, (December 1981/January 1982).

THE INSURGENT
SOCIOLOGIST

SPECIAL ISSUE
SOCIALIST TRANSITION: THEORY AND PRACTICE

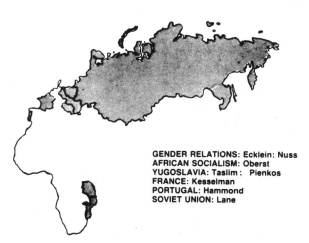

GENDER RELATIONS: Ecklein; Nuss
AFRICAN SOCIALISM: Oberst
YUGOSLAVIA: Taslim ;   Pienkos
FRANCE: Kesselman
PORTUGAL: Hammond
SOVIET UNION: Lane

POLAND SYMPOSIUM:
Szymanski;
Kostecki & Mrela;
Chhachhi, Palet & Kurian;
Angotti; Singer

The Insurgent Sociologist
C/o Department of Sociology
University of Oregon
Eugene, OR 97403

VOL. 12, NO. 1-2, WINTER-SPRING 1984, $8.00

INFOTECH AND THE THIRD WORLD

Armand Mattelart
Translated by Christopher Knee

In Africa, 7 out of 20 countries have practically no information technology ... The poorest countries have no way of paying the admission price to the infotech era, and will therefore remain excluded from the dawning new civilisation.
– M.S. Karoui, Director of the Tunisian National Information Technology Centre, speaking at the Paris Infotech Show in September 1982

All over the world, infotech is the one area invested with those beliefs and myths that so easily mistake technical revolution for a revolution in social relations. Is it not to belittle social and cultural inequalities, both nationally and internationally, to conceive of the expansion of new information technology only in terms of its beneficial social effects? Don't these inequalities predetermine the social uses which can be made of this new technological arsenal?

The sources of the mythology which sanctifies the therapeutic character of microprocessors are extremely varied. On the one hand there is the sales talk for the general public exemplified by the following publicity which appeared in the major Paris newspapers in September 1981 for a micro- and mini-computer company, and which praised the 'softness' of this technology: 'A supple infotech, like a reed which will bend in response to sudden strains; a crystal-clear infotech which guarantees transparent management; a chameleon infotech which will react quickly to changes; a finely tuned infotech like a violin which respects human sensibility...'

On the other hand there are the beliefs and proclamations illustrated by the many best sellers appearing in the last few years, such as Jean-Jacques Servan-Schreiber's *Le défi mondial* and Alvin Toffler's *The Third Wave*. With the microprocessor, the Third World could at last get its chance of development, writes Jean-Jacques Servan-Schreiber:

All those who, for almost thirty years have devoted themselves to the problems of the Third World, and who, for the most part, have chosen India in its immensity as their example, have reached the same conclusion: the strategy was wrong... What was needed and what will be needed is to emphasise *decentralisation*, to reverse all the mechanisms leading to *concentration* and blocking development. We see now how the process of informatising (*informatisation*) will lend itself to the inversion of this inhuman dynamic, by adapting locally to Third World problems and thus allowing it to begin to regain its balance...

But how, in fact, did the Third World see the arrival of information systems? The expansion of information technology – or rather the united front of information technology, telecommunications and *audiovisual*, since they are now indissoluble – comes at the right time to remind us of the multiple realities that make up the Third World, the distances which separate them from one another and from the rest of the world.

With 80% of the world population and 25% of GNPs, the Third World countries in 1980 only represented 5 to 7% of operational information systems. The USA, Japan and Western European countries held 85% of computer resources. In terms of telecommunications equipment, the Third World represented only a 10% slice of the world market. The situation as regards audiovisual equipment is of the same order: one person in every 500 either possesses or has access to a television set. No more than 20% of world radiophonic transmission and reception resources are located in the Third World. These figures reflect no more nor less than the weakness of the technological and scientific potential of these countries: 3% of spending on scientific and technological research and development, and 13% of engineers and researchers.

National Policies

Industrial infotech policy is only a part of the national strategies which are beginning to appear in the Third World. One organisation in particular has become the centre and forum of these strategies: the IBI (Intergovernmental Bureau of Informatics), which includes representatives from the many Third World governments and from some industrial nations such as France, Italy and Spain. It was at the Torremolinos Conference of 1978, organised by the IBI under the auspices of UNESCO, that there first appeared signs of a need for international consultation. The ground had been laid particularly in Latin America by a number of regional meetings of infotech authorities from most of the countries of the subcontinent. In Torremolinos, the different participants sketched the broad outlines of what they hoped would become a national infotech regulation policy: a definition of priorities for the applications of information technology, the elaboration of a computer acquisition policy, the formulation of a coherent research policy, training programmes for technicians and experts, the setting up of a national infotech industry both in hardware and in software.

The IBI member countries are far from unanimous on the application of these policies. For example, Chile, whose political economic model follows to the letter the directives of the neo-liberal economists and sees Milton Friedman as a guru, has sold off all its electronics industry and dreams of becoming a vast commercial warehouse through which would pass all the products of large foreign microelectronics firms. This does not prevent it from sticking to its national security doctrines when it comes to using its imported computers for repressive ends. This theme of national security, as indeed that of the police and military uses of information technology, is not, unfortunately, included in the discussions held by the large international organisations with governmental representation, in spite of its weighing heavily on the structure of telematic systems and determining their intro-duction in many Third World countries. This theme is only occasionally raised by humanitarian organisations devoted to the defence of human rights.

The spread of infotech does not always occur through the same institutional channels. In countries with authoritarian regimes the logic of repression is certainly the motor behind the modernisation of information systems. One has only to think of Argentina under the generals where the police force drove cars fitted with computers linked to data banks as sophisticated as those to be found in Northern Ireland. In many Third World countries, however, infotech is spread by less aggressive sectors of the state apparatus: tax collection, the judicial system, state administration, planning, the management of state industries, technical and scientific information. From this point of view, each country has its specificities that need to be uncovered. One thing, however, is certain: the electronic updating of the state does not occur in linear fashion. The differences in the degree of *informatisation* across different sectors create contradictions demonstrating that there is something new at stake: the redefinition of the relation between state and citizen, the redeployment of forms of social control. If information technology really is a qualitative shift from previous technologies, it is precisely in this area: it accompanies the restructuring of the political, economic and military apparatuses that affect the whole of society. This type of reasoning running through nation-states combines with another: that of the large transnational companies (in Third World countries) whose systems of communication between subsidiaries are at the forefront of technological innovation.

Because of their relation to earlier systems of communication (telecommunication and *audiovisual*), it is almost impossible to predict the evolution of modern information systems without taking into account the way in which previous technologies became institutionalised. Here again the Third World is far from being a unified block: differences in patterns of technological evolution; different degrees of integration into the transnational system, indicated by the presence or absence of transnational advertising agencies; different models of the implantation of radio and television, where is exists. Even when colonial and neo-colonial models have shaped radio and television models in different ways (for example the French ORTF and the BBC in Africa or commercial American television in Latin America), these have also been influenced by particular national characteristics.

It is therefore necessary to be extremely cautious when attempting to analyse the extent to which different mass audio-visual systems can absorb new technologies. It is nevertheless obvious that in those countries where the commercial model predominates, such as Brazil or Mexico, the adoption of new technologies directed at the general public will reinforce the already high degree of concentration of power in the hands of the large local multimedia conglomerates. In other cases, characterised by greater state control and by a slower growth of capital in mass cultural production, it is to be expected that the public service models will come under increasing pressure. These models are perfunctorily followed anyway since they often only serve as a transmission channel for a single political party.

In a world context, characterised by the re-emergence of the neo-liberal economic model, the mass communication apparatuses will probably not escape this logic – which decrees not only the end of the welfare state within national boundaries but also its decline in programmes of assistance and cooperation between North and South. This perspective takes us a long way from the original conception of a 'transparent' infotech, offered as a remedy to the problems of hunger, illiteracy and child mortality, and which, by ignoring national and international power relations, portrayed the introduction of computers as miraculous surgery performed on the social body.

Transnational Networks

Might a 'loss of identity' result from connecting up different national realities to the transnational telematic networks? Such initial worries appeared in parallel in certain industrialised countries and in certain Third World countries. Amongst the former, Sweden, Canada and France stand out. Amongst the latter, Brazil is the most obvious example.

In 1979, the Canadian government – particularly vulnerable because of its proximity to the USA – made a complete list of all the reasons justifying a national policy which would regulate transborder data flows. It held that the control by foreign companies over the production and processing of data ran the following risks:

1. Decreasing national control over the interruption of services resulting from technical breakdown or work stoppage.

2. Decreasing the national possibilities of protection against such things as the violation of privacy.

3. Increasing dependence on foreign experts which, at the same time, reduced the possibilities of developing human and technical resources administered in the national interest.

4. Preventing the exercise of local jurisdiction over foreign companies which operate nationally and which store and process their data outside local boundaries.

5. Undermining the national telecommunications system through the use of direct transmission satellites.

6. Allowing the publication of confidential information.

7. Giving a particularly important role to foreign data banks as well as to foreign values, products and services.

In 1979, Brazil revealed a similar set of worries and justified protectionist measures towards transnational infotech companies. Each company wishing to use foreign data banks should apply for permission from the authorities which favour the installation in Brazil of resources such as data banks or information systems. Indeed, here is the fundamental problem: even the smallest micro-terminal parachuted into the most deprived area needs to tap the whole macrostructure of its place of production. What is at stake with these multiple networks of medical, banking and meteorological data is the creation of transnational information conglomerates, the restructuring of publishing and audiovisual industries in the processing of all kinds of data.

Many Third World researchers have demonstrated the danger of the belief that access to information guarantees the democratisation of medical services, for example, and access to care. Amongst others, a report from Venezuela stated the following:

> The health, education and urban transport sectors are in such a precarious state that to talk of applying information technology to these services is madness. The hospitals are short of cotton wool, surgical spirit and bandages. In schools, overcrowding and unhygienic conditions are serious risks to the health of the children.

The promotion of medical data banks offers the temptation of plugging in to ultramodern transnational networks while completely obliterating from view the existing medical infrastructure.

In Columbia, the possibility of connecting up with the American Medlars system – which holds a virtual monopoly over world medical data – caused a clash between different factions of the medical profession. Indeed, what was recognised as natural by some, in the name of the universality of scientific and technical values, was not recognised as such by others. These were concerned to preserve their own accumulation of knowledge about Colombian aetiology; they advocated, at the same time as access to Medlars, the creation of data banks more closely adapted to the country's situation.

The demands of Third World countries concerning the control of data banks match the demands of some industrial countries, in Europe, for example. In the last few years, these latter have managed to recover ground which had been totally occupied by the USA. Even if 56% of data base and data bank systems accessible to European users are still American, as opposed to 26% of European origin, it is worth noting that there exist at present 264 European data bases and banks; these numbered only 50 at the beginning of 1980, when the Euronet data transmission network was set up, and 5 in 1975.

Third World progress in these matters is much slower, even though an increasing number of these countries are developing national policies. Witness the joint communiqué signed in 1982, after a seminar in Mexico, by the Mexican Ministry of Planning and Finance and the French interministerial group on science and technology. The signatories stated that they attached 'the greatest importance to the maintenance of each country's national identity and, in this context, to the safeguard and promotion of all languages, in particular French and Spanish, as production and communication languages in information systems'. They also noted that 'the major data bases and banks today had been conceived using criteria which, although useful for large industrialised nations, were not always adapted to the needs of developing nations'.

Microelectronics and North/South Cooperation

In an increasingly internationalising economy, the weight of international power relations asserts itself whenever certain Third World countries attempt to predict the socio-economic consequences of the spread of micro-technology in the process of production. The poorer Third World countries are worried that the spread of robotics and automated factories will cause them to lose, in the not-too-distant future, the advantages they derive at present from their cheap labour force. The various proposed solutions do not successfully allay their fears that companies will repatriate commodity production to industrialised countries in order to substitute automation for labour intensive production.

This is but one aspect of the power game being played out over the advent of new microprocessor technologies and which it is necessary to tackle if the 'North/South dialogue' is not to become merely an operation whose primary aim would be to extend the market for key industries of the North. This would otherwise do no more than endorse a new international division of labour based on the 'knowledge and information industries'.

Is this not the hidden face of the massive micro-computer export projects and of the prophetic speeches which accompany them? In an interview with a French weekly publication in June 1982, Jean-Jacques Servan-Schreiber had no hesitation in stating:

> I have often been accused of wasting my time selling computers to *nègres* [blacks]. Even from a selfish point of view and remaining at the economic level, these critics do not realise that if we succeed, it is French jobs we are defending. And if you consider not only the Africans but also the Indians, Chinese, Arabs and Latin American peasants, then I can assure you that the problem of unemployment will be solved because there will be more jobs than all the industrial countries together can fill.

Is this not totally ignoring the increasing demands that countries like India and Brazil, to name but two, are making for the control not only of the consumption of micro-technology but also of the production of hardware and software?

Nevertheless, we must recognise the tension between, on the one hand, the reindustrialisation projects of the large countries of the North based on electronic high technology, and on the other, the more egalitarian redefinition of relations with the Third World. This recognition is the necessary starting point of any debate that attempts to consider realistically the impact of new technologies on the transformation of international economic relations. Any one-sided celebration of new technologies runs the risk of being no more than sales talk.

The recent projects outlined by the French socialist government aimed at reviving French industry show clearly the contradictions which must be faced by those who, within today's international constraints, are proposing foundations for a 'new world economic order'. These contradictions are particularly obvious in strategies aimed at the electronics industry. Any way out of the crisis by means of high technology throws the country into a scheme of preferential industrial alliances. The favoured site for the internationalisation of French firms results from their need to conquer the American market: a market worth ten times that of France and half that of the world, without even counting America's technological riches. The difficulties in achieving European industrial unity – recently threatened yet again by the alliance between the Dutch multinational Philips and the American telecommunications giant, AT&T – is another element complicating any reindustrialisation plans which attempt to take account of both national independence and the emancipation of poor nations.

Editors' Note

This essay has been adapted by the Radical Science Collective from one entitled 'Informatique et Tiers-Monde'.

Bibliography

J.P. Chamoux, *Information sans frontière*, Paris, La Documentation Française, 1980.

D. Ernst, ed., *The New International Division of Labour, Technology and Under-Development*, Frankfurt/New York, Campus, 1980.

G.R.E.S.E.A., *Du télégraphe au télétexte*, Paris, Les Editions ouvrières, collection Nord/Sud, 1982.

S. Karoui, *L'Amérique, l'Europe et les autres: A la recherche de l'informatique*, Paris, Les clés du monde, 1981.

A. Madec, *Les flux transfrontières de données*, Paris, La documentation française, 1982.

A. Mattelart, *Transnationals and the Third World Struggle for Culture*, Boston. Bergin & Garvey, 1983.

A. Mattelart et H. Schmucler, *L'ordinateur et le tiers-monde: l'Amérique latine à l'heure des choix télématiques*, Paris, Maspero, 1983; published in English as *Communication and Information Systems in Latin America: Freedom to Choose?*, Norwood, NJ, Ablex, 1984.

J.J. Servan-Schreiber, *Le défi mondial*, Fayard, Paris, 1980.

A. Toffler, *The Third Wave*, Pan, 1981.

United Nations, Centre on Transnational Corporations, *Transnational Corporations and Transborder Data Flows: A Technical Paper*, NY, 1982.

Science-Fiction Studies

#34 = Volume 11, Part 3 = November 1984 • Can. $7.50
Copyright © *SFS Publications*, 1984

ARTICLES

REVIEW-ARTICLES

BOOKS IN REVIEW   NOTES AND CORRESPONDENCE

New and renewal subscriptions for 1985 must be sent to Prof. R.M. Philmus, English Dept., Concordia University, 7141 Sherbrooke St. W., Montréal, Québec, Canada H4B 1R6. Cheques or money orders should be made payable to *SFS Publications*.

	Via Surface Mail		Via Air Mail
	Individuals	Institutions	
In Canada	Can. $ 14.50	Can. $ 22.00	For Air Mail
In the USA	US $ 12.50	US $ 19.00	add US $5.00
Overseas	US $ 14.50	US $ 21.50	

HIGH-TECH ALTERNATIVISM
The Case of the Community Memory Project

Tom Athanasiou

David Noble recently argued, in the now-defunct *democracy* magazine, that 'the fight for alternatives ... diverts attention from the realities of power and technological development, holds out facile and false promises, and reinforces the cultural fetish for technological transcendence'.[1] I'd like to agree and yet take issue with Noble's conclusion – that political activists concerned with science and technology should concentrate almost exclusively on strategies of opposition to new technologies.

Anti-technological confrontation is crucial, but alone it cannot support the development of a stronger and more sophisticated technology-control movement. Confrontation should be judged as much by its success in catalyzing larger cultural and political shifts as by its immediate effectiveness in blocking technologies of passivity and death.

The point is not to stop 'technology', but to make and enforce different choices about it.[2] The popular political culture that can inform such choices will be built not only from the passion of refusal; it must express as well the widespread fascination with modern technology. Only when that fascination is brought up against the dark side of today's technological constructions will we have in hand the core elements of a new technical culture.

Many technologies have been passed over, ignored and suppressed in the last few hundred years. The alternatives movement of the 60s and 70s concentrated, for good reasons, on demonstrating the viability of alternative approaches within the relatively low-tech worlds of energy production and agriculture.

Today this will not do; the environmental sensibilities of the 1970s have been overrun by neo-liberal 'tough-mindedness'. Opportunistic theories of 're-industrialization' have colonized the political spaces opened up a decade earlier by movements with far more substantive intentions. Today the alternatives movement, if it is to remain politically relevant, must find itself anew in the debates about computerization.[3]

The microchip is nothing if not flexible. Applications abound, but capital will pursue only those which show promise of profit, or which provide for more efficient systems of control. It will continue to repress those potentials which run counter to its overall logic of commodification and pacification.

One of these potentials is the development of a 'de-massified' mass-media. Such media would be based upon the integration of computer technology into electronic communications systems in such a way as to support a wide range of active individual initiatives. They could provide for the elimination of the distinction between producers and consumers of information, encourage public conversations and, by virtue of being embedded within community social institutions, empower rather than pacify their users.

If we ever make it out of the historical cul-de-sac of capitalist society, such media as this will certainly play a role in the organization of public life.[4] Still, their present value is a matter of some uncertainty, and is consistently overstated by its proponents. Certainly it is true that computer communications is widely described as 'revolutionary' by many who hardly have the end of institutionalized domination in mind. Like solar technology in the 1970s, the notion of democratic computer communications attracts more than its share of the politically tame. Nevertheless, the liberatory potential of solar power will not be realized during the Age of Capital, and the same is true of information technology. The impulse to develop non-hierarchical communications systems (not market-oriented videotex systems) contains a real moment of rebellion against the hierarchical logic that today dominates technical design.

The Community Memory Project

Community Memory is a system for the public management of public information. It is an open channel for community communications and information exchange, and a way for people with common interests to find each other... All of the information in the Community Memory is put in directly by the people who use the system: anyone can post messages, read any of the other communications that are there, and add comments or suggestions at any time.[5]

The Community Memory Project in Berkeley is an attempt to build and deploy such a non-hierarchical computer communications system. I have been active in the project for many years and have developed strong opinions about both its efficacy and its history. This article reflects those opinions more than any group consensus, though it has been read by many others, and I fancy that most would agree with the bulk of it.

Conceiving of such a project is relatively simple; carrying that conception into reality is a different matter. The execution would take a lot of time, energy and money: large software projects are very expensive to develop even when the results are very cheap. The founders knew this and tried to take it into account. They decided to proceed by writing the underlying 'system software' in as modular a way as possible – in effect implementing the Community Memory system on a generalized text/data handling 'toolkit' that could support commercial spin-offs as well as Community Memory itself. These spinoffs wouldn't take much time, and they'd provide the reams of cash necessary to support the system. So the story of Community Memory is really two stories, reflecting our history as a political/technical collective that took a long, unplanned, and largely unpleasant trip through the computer industry.

Only in the last year have we actually completed an advanced prototype of the Community Memory system itself. (The first three public terminals became operational in Berkeley in August of 1984.) Consequently, our experience can hardly be the basis of overblown generalizations about high-tech alternativism; we've learned only how difficult it is to beat capitalism on its own terms. We've little experience in actually operating a non-hierarchical communications system. We don't know yet whether our efforts were worth the trouble. We may never know – nor agree among ourselves.

People, Places, Things

Community Memory has been jokingly referred to as a 'closely-held collective'. Simultaneously a political organization and a systems software shop, and run by the active participants in an endless series of open meetings, it nevertheless maintains a legal structure which restricts ultimate power to the active 'members'. We have voted only twice, yet these votes were significant. They

How To **Browse Titles**

Step 1 Press  FIND

INDEX

ADD

EXIT

Step 2

Use the up & down arrow buttons
to position the highlight on a title.

↑

↓

MESSAGE TITLES (Newest to oldest)

(752 messages found)

752. energy fools the magician
751. WE HAVE TO REGISTER PEOPLE TO VOTE
750. nunce fui sorcai ni a avido plumage mas ordinario
749. Volvo station wagon -- for sale CHEAP
748. technical aid to Nicaragua
747. Vintage LunchBoxes bought or sold
746. Cartoon ideas wanted
745. Bike-Run-Walk Jolon CA to San Miguel CA Oct.7
744. Upcoming events at La Pena
743. Suggestions to improve Communi'. Memory

To read the message, press   Y
                             E
                             S

And there's the message:

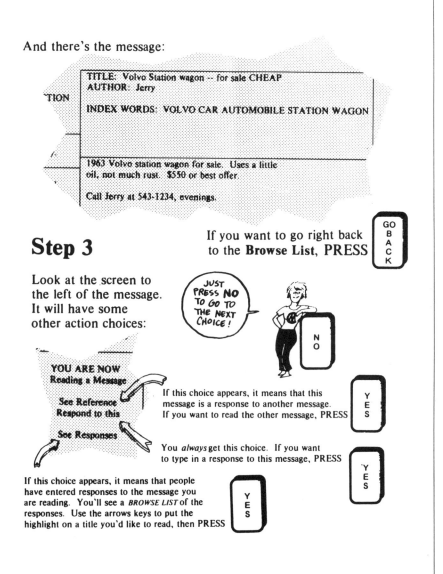

TITLE: Volvo Station wagon -- for sale CHEAP
AUTHOR: Jerry

INDEX WORDS: VOLVO CAR AUTOMOBILE STATION WAGON

1963 Volvo station wagon for sale. Uses a little oil, not much rust. $550 or best offer.

Call Jerry at 543-1234, evenings.

Step 3

If you want to go right back to the **Browse List**, PRESS

`GO BACK`

Look at the screen to the left of the message. It will have some other action choices:

JUST PRESS **NO** TO GO TO THE NEXT CHOICE!

`NO`

YOU ARE NOW Reading a Message

See Reference

Respond to this

If this choice appears, it means that this message is a response to another message. If you want to read the other message, PRESS

`YES`

See Responses

You *always* get this choice. If you want to type in a response to this message, PRESS

`YES`

If this choice appears, it means that people have entered responses to the message you are reading. You'll see a *BROWSE LIST* of the responses. Use the arrows keys to put the highlight on a title you'd like to read, then PRESS

`YES`

reflected antagonisms rooted in our ill-fated venture into commercial software production.

While we've barely succeeded in finishing the first cut of the Community Memory system, we have managed to become a well-known and frequently-cited populist computing center. And through close association with the publisher of a respected (if small-circulation and infrequently published) journal, the *Journal of Community Communications*,[6] we've had some success in broadening the typical critique of information technology to include communications issues.

Tuesday night dinner/meetings are usually attended by about a dozen, but there are altogether about twenty 'friends of Community Memory'. We are writers, still using some of the Left's first word processors. We are programmers who would rather not work for the military – or the banks. We are ecology and peace activists. We are ex-hippy marginals now earning good wages as technical writers. We have become alternative communications experts; one of us even has a degree that says so. We are, as a group, sharp, scientific and articulate. We even have our own sociologist, a lucid and funny fellow from the UC Berkeley sociology department that has been 'studying' the project for several years now.

All this to do again what had already been done. In 1973 a small group of technologically astute activists in San Francisco put up a small three-terminal Community Memory system and kept it up for about fourteen months. Uses reflected the locations of the terminals. One was in a music store and collected information about gigs, bands and the like. Another, at a hippy hardware store, specialized in Alternative Technology and barter. The third, located in a public library in the Mission District, a poor area of San Francisco, was little more than a high-tech graffiti board.

The experiment was pronounced a success, but attempts to raise the funds to expand and continue it proved a failure. Years later a group including some of the original founders decided that conditions had changed enough to justify another, more ambitious, pilot project. This meant writing the software from scratch, and writing it to run on the new generations of super-microcomputers that had become available in the interim. The new system would be powerful, sophisticated and, most of all, portable. It could be replicated again and again, in different neighborhoods in different cities. Or it could be used by 'non-geographical communities' of people who had specific needs for a dynamic shared information pool, e.g. community organizers from different regions. All this would be possible because the new system would eventually tie individual Community Memory Systems together into one grand 'network'.

Pacific Software

When we failed to find a marketing company already in existence, we looked to our own circle for people to handle our commercial spinoffs. In this context the fact that we could count among our friends several successful inventors and small-scale entrepreneurs was seen as an asset. Our friends would found a software company, Pacific Software, to which Community Memory would license its goods in the hope of earning royalties to help fund its public programs. Community Memory itself would be protected from commercial entanglements and we could blithely proceed as left-libertarian information activists. Everyone would be a winner.

For the record, the commercial spinoffs we developed were:
1) Sequitur, a sophisticated 'relational' database management system built upon the Community Memory 'toolkit'. Designed to run on small computers, it is distinguished by the high degree of integration that it achieves between text and data processing.
2) X.Dot, a portable C-language implementation of an international standard data-communications protocol, X.25. This is the foundation upon which communication between independent Community Memory systems will be based.

The disinterested observer will perhaps not be surprised to learn that matters did not proceed as smoothly as we had imagined, and that our subsequent organizational development reflected the contradictions of our political, technical and entrepreneurial entanglements. To some extent, this was anticipated, but we overestimated our ability to manage the contradictions. Years after we began technical development, we have only barely managed to get a functioning Community Memory System out the door.

For the collective, commercial pressure became a mutagenic, almost fatal force. Nor did our friends do well as capitalists. We, for our part, seriously underestimated the market pressures which would keep us from making a fortune and quickly exiting. Pacific Software, for its part, made the situation worse by proving incapable of proper planning and scheduling. There were always changes to be made to the code, always more features that the market demanded. And providing them remained, for far too long,

Sequitur™
... So flexible, it may be all the software you need.

Sequitur™
... Database management and word processing in one system.

Here's Why:

Everything happens on the screen. You use the same screen editing techniques everywhere. Moving the cursor around just as you would with any word processor, you fill in step-by-step prompts to:

- Set up your tables
- Enter and edit your data
- Select, sort, join, and otherwise combine your data to discover new information and new relationships
- Generate mailing lists and print form letters
- Perform calculations and print reports

Sequitur offers fully integrated editing. With Sequitur you can edit any part of a table. Once you edit it, Sequitur makes the change throughout the database, wherever that information is stored.

But you don't lose the data you began with. If you change your mind, you can bring back earlier versions with a single keystroke. There's nothing like it on the market at any price.

Sequitur is fully relational. You don't have to know exactly how you want to organize your data before you enter it. Sequitur will do it for you afterward, letting you rearrange and retrieve data at will, in all kinds of relationships.

Sequitur offers unprecedented versatility: data entry, database management, word processing, report generation, form letters, preprinted forms, mailing lists, document management, and more in a single system.

the responsibility of reluctant Community Memory programmers. Meanwhile, Pacific Software went broke.

In retrospect, our collective was organizationally inadequate to the tasks it set itself. Power relations, and with them lines of responsibility, were too informal to adequately replace the managerial mechanisms by which traditional capitalist firms direct operations. Not that they were entirely informal: the small 'junta' of long-term and ideologically committed members could not pass without notice; besides, they paid the bills. But since their authority was neither embodied within formal organizational relations nor considered legitimate, it could never be decisively exercised.

We eventually adopted a committee structure, with a 'co-ordinating committee' empowered to manage but not set policy, but by then it was fairly late in the game. Our formative years were spent toiling under 'the tyranny of structurelessness', a tyranny that obscured crucial realities within a haze of emotionally charged and even arbitrary authority. Personnel disputes could consume tremendous blocks of meeting time and yet remain unresolved. Technical reviews of code were constrained by the impossibility of staff changes. Accountability was vague, with all decisions subject to perpetual renegotiation. Long-term planning was simply impossible. And day by day, market pressures grew.

South Africa and the Naval Surface Weapons Laboratory

We anticipated that capitalist relations would press against our democratic ideals. Yet our anticipation was vague and not really to the point. When reality caught up with us, we were startled by its brazenness.

About three years ago, X.Dot was finally ready to sell. Pacific Software was trying to establish it in the telecommunications market, and we all had great hopes. (At the time we were asking about $300,000 per copy.) But when Pacific finally landed a customer it was a company in Johannesburg – they were building an airline reservation system and needed an X.25.

We refused the sale, then went on to a complex and difficult debate that led to our prohibition of sales to South Africa. (Sales to Eastern Bloc countries were already prohibited by the government.) We also developed a method of restricting sales to the military by limiting Pacific Software's sublicensing rights to 'commercial and non-proprietary' applications.

Though none among us wanted to make a sale to South Africa, the discussions were complex and tense; the beginning of

the end of our naiveté. Only one person, who felt that we needed
the sale to establish X.Dot in the market, was willing to argue for it.
The argument was raised that Israel was as bad as South Africa
(indeed the two countries have jointly developed a variety of
nuclear arms) but was defeated in the name of political realism.
After all, there is an international technology boycott against
South Africa, but not against other unsavory states like Israel. We
even considered allowing Pacific Software to make the sale and
donating our share to the liberation movement in South Africa.
But when contacted, a front group for the African national
Congress refused the support, preferring to forego the funds and
deny South Africa the technology.

I, along with others, opposed the sale on the grounds of its
unique benefit to South Africa. X.Dot, designed to be easily
transportable among a variety of machines, would have been
especially useful to South Africa, suffering as it does a technological boycott of some significance. This same criterion of
uniqueness led me to support sales of Sequitur to the military,
when not much later they became an issue.

It was the disagreement over these sales that first emerged as
open conflict. In the absence of the clear-cut ethical/political
imperative provided by a pre-existing boycott, unanimity broke
down. There was reason to doubt, whatever sales we denied
ourselves, that our denial would have an effect. Sequitur was of no
unique benefit to anyone; there were dozens of systems that could
do the job equally well (perhaps better). Furthermore, there was a
strong feeling that, whatever military sales policy we were
eventually to adopt, it would be necessary to keep it quiet. The
logic of the market, many felt, dictated that we not endanger
Pacific Software by making it appear political or constrained in
undefined ways.

Our shared understandings were breaking down. Just what
was so different between doing business with the military and
doing business with the banks – between fast death and slow
death? In the absence of a willingness to make a public statement,
and considering the onerous uses to which information management systems like Sequitur were put in the commercial world, such
distinctions as could be made failed to win easy consensus.
Instead, the military debate became the locus of expression for
more generalized antagonisms rooted in the political and
interpersonal ambiguities of the larger venture.

With the system itself so far from realization, it could only
enter our calculations as an abstraction. Anti-military initiatives,
in contrast, were very much part of the political environment. The

military debate was fertile ground for an organizational crisis for exactly this reason; it forced an end to the easy assumption of political efficacy. The value of the project now had to be weighed against more concrete realities.

Just why was Community Memory a valuable political project anyway? Was it because it would try to demonstrate that high technology could be used to counter social alienation? Was it because by doing something we would be taken seriously even in the pragmatist nightmare of modern America? Was it our institutional existence itself that was important – that a few lost souls of the computer state would hear of us and know they were not alone? Was it because we were struggling with radical collectivism? Or would the system itself justify our small contribution to capitalist modernization?

It was a long debate and many claims were made. Of them all, one seems, in retrospect, particularly problematic – the claim that 'all money is dirty money'. I supported this position myself, and argued that the market would squeeze us dearly for our silent protest. In the end I was over-ruled, and have come to be glad for it. The abstract consistency that I wanted had no place in the contradictory reality we had stumbled into. I remember it now as determined as much by frustration as by political considerations themselves.

Labor Process, Work Identity, Democracy

Programming labor always held a special status at Community Memory. Despite occasional conscious and semi-conscious attempts to value non-technical work more highly, the logic of the project itself imposed the centrality of programming labor. In the last instance, it was the success or failure of the programmers that would determine the success or failure of the venture as a whole.

As technical development became absurdly protracted, the social consequences of the situation emerged more clearly. We fought the tendency for non-programming staff to become mere support staff for the programmers; such a situation would have been intolerable, especially since only one of the women was a programmer. But we were never able to break the hegemony of technical work over the project as a whole. Worse, the larger group never managed to get control of the design process. It was 'technical decisions' made by programmers, decisions about arcana like program capabilities and software development strategies, that led us all into the labyrinth.

And the programmers group was not without its problems; we had our own meetings, our own work process, and our own struggle with the old guard. During the early days we established a design process based on an odd mix of extreme hierarchy and participatory democracy. One of the founders, Mr. X., played the role of 'chief programmer' in our democratic appropriation of the traditional 'chief programmer team'.[7] The rest of us, programmers of various skill levels, played indians. Mr. X. came up with basic designs; we discussed, criticized, redesigned and coded them.

To a large degree it worked: we were able to appropriate the broadly varied skills and predilections of individual programmers within a design/implementation process that both preserved the thematic unity of design (Mr. X. did most of it) and allowed for genuine participation and learning on the part of those not playing the role of 'chief programmer'.

But as time went on and pressure mounted, the tenuousness of our accommodation became more manifest. Mr. X. lost his commitment to pedagogy and his willingness to have others challenge his designs. Further, he became increasingly unwilling to stop designing and to work towards a final artefact. Others, myself included, found ourselves increasingly in the role of technical managers: trying to impose schedules and account-ability, maintain a functional programming environment, and continue to integrate and debug the system as a whole. Others refused responsibility altogether.

I mention all this to underscore the fragility of our democracy. We were able to subsume skill differences within co-operative relations, but the understandings within which we did so were not robust enough to survive the long campaign. Here too, as in the larger group, the insufficiency of our work democracy manifested itself in the breakdown in personal relationships. Some of us were, of course, more trouble than others, but these contingencies of personality were the means by which the inadequacies of our process manifested itself; they were not the causes themselves.

In the end, Mr. X. and two of his closest compatriots left the group. Those of us who remained were largely in agreement about what had happened and why, so it's no surprise that we were able to continue to work together. Indeed, with the departure of our most design-oriented member, we were finally able to concentrate on the more prosaic, but now absolutely crucial task of finishing the programs.

It's taken me some time to achieve a reasonable perspective on these events. I remain unsure of the relationship between our programmer team/work collective and more the typical forms of technical work organization. Many assure me that there is no difference at all, and that many, if not most, programming projects are run as loosely as was ours. I remain unsure.

Certainly our articulated commitment to participatory democracy made for significant ideological differences, and certainly too our programmer/manager relations were somewhat atypical. But are there deeper similarities? Non-Taylorist forms of organization have often been found necessary in skilled technical work, so we can claim no uniqueness here. And what of the 'family feeling' so many Silicon Valley firms strive to cultivate among their staffs? Wasn't our 'collective' analogous here as well?

A really severe interpretation of Community Memory's history would reveal even more disturbing parallels with typical high-tech paternalism. Instead of management we had 'the Junta'. Like management they kept organizational goals firmly in mind; like Dad they defined the norms by which the children were judged. And like typical professional workers, we worked as much for our identities as for our articulated goals. Like a position in the typical corporate family, a job at Community Memory came complete with a sense of place. Only in this case that sense was defined not in the terms of fast-lane achievement culture, but against them. We were radical engineers, community designers, people's programmers.

Who Cares about Democratic Communications Anyway?

Today, five years after the reincarnation of Community Memory, it's obvious that our fund-raising strategy didn't work out quite as planned. But it did make sense at the time, and our lack of luck with it doesn't mean other groups elsewhere couldn't do better. But one warning is certainly appropriate: we thought ourselves very sophisticated, but we failed to be sophisticated enough to manage the pressures of the market. Given enough time, we will see forms of work-democracy far in advance of any existing today. But will they exist and prosper under the regime of Capital? Our experience indicates that they will not.

We have accomplished something of our original goals. We've done a lot of writing and gotten a lot of publicity. Perhaps we've even had some small effect on the norms by which computer communications systems will be judged. The first version of the system is working fine in our shop, and by the time this article sees publication the terminals will be out: one in a community center, one in a general store, one in the Berkeley Co-op. Beyond that our future is unwritten.

Conclusion

Community Memory's stated and most obvious goal is to demonstrate that computer information systems can be built that will help people to meet other people with similar interests, in effect to create an electronic public space. This modest intent is not anti-capitalist, except in that manner that all 'useful utopias' are, by invoking concrete images of alternative futures, thus making the end of this miserable world more easily imaginable.

The intention of this essay has been to argue for the importance of an alternativist aspect within the larger technology movement, and to trace the history of one benighted attempt to make that argument in practice. It should not be read as an overstated plea for an 'alternativist' politics, for such a politics will certainly fail if left on its own.

Within the present ideological climate, it's very difficult to project a concept of technology that is both visionary and critical. Community Memory is important because it tries to do just that. It is visionary because it demonstrates, in a concrete way, that we can design new technologies to serve our own chosen ends. It is critical because it contrasts itself with the productions of the telecommunications corporations, and challenges their reduction of human social interaction to the passive consumption of information commodities.

This is an odd moment in human history. It is difficult to imagine a revolution without hope, and today hope requires the healing of not only nature, but technics as well. Somehow the refusal of capitalist technology must simultaneously affirm the possibility of shaping tools to other purposes.

Notes

1. 'Present Tense Technology' was printed in three parts, in the Spring, Summer and Fall 1983 issues of *democracy*. It demands reading, for in a period characterized by a rather blithe leftist realpolitik, Noble calls for a focus on the simple truths of social power and class antagonism. His assertion – that the 'friends of labor' disarm the working class by exaggerating the possibilities for workplace technologic reform – must be taken seriously. Still, this article will take a more agnostic position, reflecting as it does the author's inability to imagine a modern radical technology movement without an alternativist dimension.

2. In this regard the women's 'pro-choice' movement is perhaps an evocative model of a social movement that, while concerned with

technology (in this case medical technology), is oriented more towards new options than to direct opposition. (When it comes to abortion, it's the right that's 'anti-tech'.) The 'choice' issues raised for pregnant women, in significant part by the availability of technological options, highlight cultural and political dilemmas which cannot be addressed by simple opposition. In many cases (e.g. nuclear power) simple opposition is clearly the appropriate response to capitalist technological innovation, but with regard to micro-electronic and biological technologies it will not do.

3.   High-tech alternativism carries with it the danger of strengthening science-based ideologies of 'progress'. Such ideologies, eroded over the last few decades by the insanity of heavy-metal capitalism, threaten a resurgence in the guise of the 'micro-electronic revolution'. The constantly insinuated image of the micro as toy, helpmate and liberator has the effect of rejuvenating technologic wonder as a crucial element in the systems of social apologism. As is usual whenever the mass imagination is riveted to the gleam of the latest trinkets, capital benefits.

On the other hand, any politics of technology that declines to focus exclusively on opposition must propose alternatives to systems designed and implemented around the imperatives of Capital. Co-optation is no danger as long as nuclear war, or technologically structured pacification, or the corporate production of cancer, remains the focus of attention. But attempts to define alternative models of industrial automation, for example attempts which are becoming increasingly popular among left economists (Cooley, Shaiken and Melman, just for starters) – must risk absorption into the same sort of humanistic high-tech ideology that confronts Community Memory.

4.   For a relatively recent example, see the 'Kenner' network in the leftist utopian novel by Marge Piercy, *Woman on the Edge of Time*, NY, Fawcett, 1976.

5.   From 'An Introduction to Community Memory', available for $1 from Community Memory, 916 Parker Street, Berkeley, CA 94710.

6.   The *Journal of Community Communications* (available from Village Design, P.O. Box 996, Berkeley, CA 94701) is a small, infrequent quarterly that focuses on the theory and practice of 'non-hierarchical communications'. Many, but by no means all, of the articles are related to computer communications. Coffee-houses in 16th century London, a Lakota Indian radio station, pornographic software, Control Data Corporations' venture into Appropriate Technology and Punk Rock have all found space in recent issues.

7.   In a traditional 'chief programming team' the work process is organized to maximize the productivity of one super-programmer, by factoring off as much of his (sic) work as possible. The chief-programmer will do all the design, and most of the programming, but he will have 'coders' to which he can assign fully specified sub-modules. The team will also contain a librarian, a secretary, a hardware support person, a backup chief programmer, etc.

The Berkeley Journal of Sociology

A Critical Review   Volume XXIX 1984

Terry Strathman on **Child-Rearing and Utopia**

Martin Gilens on **The Gender Gap**

Denise Segura on **Labor Market Stratification and Chicanas**

Jennifer Pierce on **Functionalism and Chicano Family Research**

Jeff Holman on **Underdevelopment Aid**

James Jasper on **Art and Politics**

Individuals: $5.00   Discounts on Back Issues
Institutions: $12.00   and Multi-Volume Orders

THE BERKELEY JOURNAL OF SOCIOLOGY
Univ. of CA   458A Barrows Hall   Berkeley, CA 94720

COMMUNITY RADIO IN BRITAIN: Reach Out and Touch Everyone

Richard Barbrook

> It has been said, and rightly so, that for the first time in history a revolution could have been made without recourse to arms. And people have pointed out that one of the first steps we should have taken, and failed to take, was to capture the radio stations. (Cohn-Bendit, p. 71)

This article arises out of the author's involvement in the community radio movement over the past few years. This campaign wishes to set up community radio stations in Britain. Such stations would give access to groups and individuals who

Mike and Lepke get the carnival on the air – 1984 Notting Hill Carnival, London

photo: *The Times*

wish to broadcast. They would seek to involve both broadcasters and listeners in the cooperative management of stations. It could be predicted such a demand would meet with hostility from the vested interests entrenched in the BBC, IBA and Home Office. But community radio supporters find themselves under attack from many on the Left as well. As recently as April 1984, the Campaign for Press and Broadcasting Freedom voted at its AGM against resolutions supporting community radio. Obviously the Campaign's idea of 'broadcasting freedom' does not include the freedom of community radio stations to broadcast! This article will look not just at the history of the community radio in Britain. It will show also how the practice of such stations challenges the theoretical nostrums held dear by many on the Left. For, as Marx calls to our attention in the VIII Thesis on Feurbach, 'all social life is essentially *practical*. All mysteries which lead theory to mysticism find their rational solution in human practice and in the comprehension of this practice.' (Marx, 1977; p. 122)

The Left and the Mass Media

Increasingly, the British Left has found itself in confrontation with the mass media. It has objected to the open hostility found in the media's output both to the Labour movement and to oppressed social groups, such as women, gays and the ethnic minorities. It has attacked the concentration of ownership in the newspaper industry and the lack of accountability in the broadcasting institutions. It has been worried by the social implications of the introduction of new technology in publishing and broadcasting.

The mass media are the most powerful means of communication between those engaged in political and trade union activity with the rest of society. Therefore the representation of socialist ideas and struggles in the media is of key importance to the Labour movement. Continuous attacks on the personalities and organisations of the Left are an obstacle to winning mass support from the populace. At the hands of the Thatcher government, both the Labour Party and the trade unions have suffered a number of defeats. Especially since the 1983 General Election, this has been attributed in part to the support given to the Tories by the mass media. Studies have examined how this takes place (Glasgow University Media Group). Other work has shown how key political issues are systematically misrepresented, such as the war in Ireland (Campaign for Free Speech on Ireland). Through the experience of the Greenham Common Peace Camp, striking trade unionists or the GLC, the Left has learnt how the media can orchestrate a hate campaign against it. Few would disagree with Tony Benn's assessment on the media's part in defeating Peter Tatchell's attempt to become MP for Bermondsey:

> ... he was hunted down and liquidated by the media, using techniques with which we are now getting familiar: misrepresentation, distortion and harassment, followed by opinion polls to check the effectiveness of the propaganda barrage . . . All those respectable TV programmes could then join in by quoting the gutter press and interviewing people on the streets to confirm the polls (Benn, 1983).

Striking miners picketing in Nottinghamshire showed how they agreed with this view by attacking TV camera crews!

The Left has attributed a wider social role to the media. It is seen as orchestrating a moral backlash against the social freedoms gained in the 1960s (Hall et al.). Those not conforming to the white, male, middle class, heterosexual world-view of the programme controllers or editors find themselves presented in clichéd roles and stock situations. There has been pressure to produce positive images of blacks, women, workers and gays. Failure to do so reinforces prejudices based on class, race, gender or sexuality (Local Radio Workshop, 1982).

In the newspaper industry, its anti-socialist bias is attributed to the ownership of most of Fleet Street by multinational corporations and rich individuals. Given their other business interests and the reliance by newspapers on corporate advertising, it is not surprising that the press is pro-capitalist. What is more, there is a newspaper oligopoly of control that restricts comment within the bourgeois consensus. This is best illustrated by the control of four national newspapers by one man, Rupert Murdoch (Murdock and Golding; Campaign for Press Freedom, 1979). The lack of accountability can be seen, too, in those institutions that are publicly regulated or controlled. The Board of Governors of the BBC and IBA are drawn from a narrow group of the 'great and good'. This is reflected in the social attitudes of those who are allowed to become programme-makers. Little or no control or access is allowed to groups lying outside this charmed circle of the professionals and the Establishment (Hood; Heller; Goodman).

Commercial interests make themselves felt in all sections of the mass media either through direct control by private interests or by the aping of their methods by public institutions. Therefore the market is seen not only as a corrupting influence in society, but also as inevitably in control of any technological change. This view has shaped the Left's opposition in practice to the further expansion of the mass media. Trade unions may be motivated by the threat to their members' jobs. But socialist commentators seem to be more concerned with the further subsumption of the mass media to the private market. This makes the likelihood that the mass media will be 'fair' to the Left even more unlikely (Local Radio Workshop; CSE Communications Group; Garnham).

Confusion in the Left

A damning critique of bourgeois society is the distinguishing feature of any socialist analysis. The problems start to arise when solutions must be offered – especially if they reveal the limitations of the original approach. A classic example is the question of censorship. When Rowland tries to make the *Observer* follow an editorial policy subject to his commercial interests, every socialist can be outraged. Traditionally, the Left fights for a loosening of controls to allow a wider diversity of views to be heard. But are all views and opinions socially acceptable? Do socialists agonise about racists and fascists being denied their right to self-expression? Feminists have demanded the social control over the distribution of sexist material, especially pornography. Thus the Left is placed in a quandary by the Bright 'Video Nasties' Bill: is it a worthy measure to outlaw sadistic films or an erosion of civil liberties? 'Emerging social groups which try to harness the new technology to their more controversial causes will find themselves bedevilled by delay, expense, and straightforward censorship of ideas not deemed suitable for discussion in the home' (Robertson).

The ambiguity arises from the issue being not just censorship, but state regulation and control. It is difficult to attack the former while supporting state interventionism. The Campaign for Press and Broadcasting Freedom presses for a 'right of reply' to defamatory copy. This involves the statutory regulation of the content of newspapers to ensure they are 'fair' and 'unbiased', with redress when they are not (Campaign for Press Freedom 1981). Recently the police have used the obscenity legislation to prosecute Airlift Comics as 'corrupting'. It takes little imagination to see that a 'right of reply' would be vigorously enforced in *Tribune* or *Socialist Action*, but not in the *Sun* or *Mail*!

The belief in government regulation reveals a wider naiveté about the role of the state. Vincent Hanna of BBC 2 *Newsnight* tried to orchestrate an Alliance bandwagon against the Labour Party during the Chesterfield by-election – and the BBC is a public corporation. Yet many on the Left (Garnham; Local Radio

Workshop; CPBF; Labour Party) support the defence of state control and regulation. As Connell commented on Garnham 1983, '... he would have the left defend, not the practice so much as an *ideal* of, "public service" broadcasting. This idealism is somewhat surprising from one usually so explicit about his commitment to marxist materialism' (Connell, p. 71). This 'idealism' results from the contradiction between the belief in a state-run economy and the reality of living under a Tory government and bourgeois bureaucracy.

It was this contradiction that was so cruelly revealed at the Campaign for Press and Broadcasting Freedom AGM. The cynical could see the rejection of open-access, co-operatively managed radio stations as a successful piece of lobbying by BBC unions afraid of the effect of competition on their members' jobs. But it is doubtful whether such arguments will inhibit the establishment of a Labour daily seeking to drive Tory papers out of the marketplace. What the CPBF wants to defend is the idealised vision of public service broadcasting. Yet there are numerous social groups outside their organisation seeking access to or redress from the mass media. One thing is certain; they do not see the BBC even as a potential solution to their grievances!

'Iskra' and the Mass Media

The demand for community radio does not only challenge the vested interests of media professionals to preserve their position. It also questions the political practice and theory of the Left in the mass media. The party newspaper is *the* main form of political organisation in the revolutionary Left. This form of political practice, traditionally associated with the ultra-left, now encompasses the whole Labour movement, including 'Leninist'-type groupings within the Labour Party (e.g. *Militant, Socialist Action, Socialist Organiser, Workers Power, Labour Herald, Chartist*).

Lenin created the Bolshevik party from the sellers and readers of *Iskra* and *Pravda* (Lenin, 1975). The various Leninist groups have tried to mimic this strategy by basing themselves around party periodicals. This is not simply a technique of revolutionary mobilisation. It represents the way a cadre of intellectuals can seek to lead the proletariat. The vanguard party uses its newspaper as the transmission belt for socialist ideas. In this view, revolutionary consciousness is brought to the working class through, in part, reading the party literature. This is a classic elitist view of the working class as incapable of self-activity and in need of guidance by intellectuals. The quality of the mental labour embodied in party publications determines each group's claim to leadership. Not surprisingly, this becomes an obsession with *what* is said, at the expense of how it is produced. Moreover, each newspaper-party dreams of becoming the party-state.

The reification of the products of intellectual labour into the 'party-line' takes on a new dimension after a revolution under conditions of state capitalism; state censorship is celebrated as part of the suppression of 'capitalism':

'Down with non-partisan writers! Down with literary supermen! Literature must become *part* of the common cause of the proletariat, "a cog and screw" of one single great Social-Democratic mechanism set in motion by the entire politically-conscious vanguard of the entire working class' (Lenin, 1979; p. 180).

The *Iskra* tradition affects the non-Leninist Left as well. *Radical Science Journal* itself sees the magazine as the means to connect the intelligentsia with the wider community of scientific workers – and to give leadership on pressing questions. This theoretical model may be a satisfactory abstraction of pre-revolutionary Russia. But it is doubtful whether it is adequate today. For instance, the primacy given to the written word does not fit into the world of the electronic media. It is noticeable that the Campaign for Press and Broadcasting Freedom began as the Campaign for *Press* Freedom only! Yet capitalism has restructured the mass media both in its social forms and technological base since the beginning of the century. Leninist theory and practice remains frozen in time as the newspaper-party. Self-styled Marxists forget Marx's own words about the capitalist mode of production:

> The bourgeoisie cannot exist without constantly revolutionising the instruments of production, and thereby the relations of production, and with them the whole relations of society . . . Constant revolutionising of production, uninterrupted disturbance of all social conditions, everlasting uncertainty and agitation distinguish the bourgeois epoch from all earlier ones . . . All that is solid melts into air . . . (Marx, 1965; pp. 36–37).

Challenges to the Leninist View

The Leninist newspaper-party sees the existing public sector broadcasting institutions as potential instruments of the party-state. This means such a theory and practice is under attack from a number of developments.

● The threat of 'privatisation' of existing broadcasting institutions and the commercial development of any new services (Thomas; Cooper; Adam Smith Institute). The defence of the existing services concedes the ideological initiative to the Tories. Free-marketeers can invoke the Millean precepts of cultural pluralism achieved through commercial competition. This allows them to mobilise the real desire of producers and consumers for greater diversity in the mass media. To dismiss their proposals as capitalist utopianism in the age of media multinationals misses their real social appeal. If the expansion of television and radio are simply opposed, then the Left seems to have nothing positive to offer beyond further (unpopular) state control.

● The re-emergence of pirate radio stations and the possibility of pirate television. Mass civil disobedience by 'breakers' forced the Home Office to find vacant frequencies for C.B. radio. This was despite previous claims that such a concession was impossible. Therefore it is not surprising that direct action has emerged in radio broadcasting. Radio piracy produces an ambivalent response in the Establishment. The

Radio Caroline

commercial radio stations and Radio 1 owe their existence to the activities of the North Sea pirates of the 1960s. Their romantic image was established not just through their popularity with the listeners; they had also the backing of a section of the Conservative Party and major commercial interests (Local Radio Workshop, 1983; pp. 3-22). The reappearance of radio piracy thus evoked a contradictory response. While the Home Office chased the pirates and the BBC/IBA hierarchies disapproved, their own stations gave them publicity. The new wave of pirates was drawn from ham radio enthusiasts and electronic hobbyists. They could set up land-based pirates because of the falling price of electronic components. No longer could a radio station be set up only after a large capital investment. By 1981, transmitters could be bought for £150-250 from home constructors. Radio Andromeda in Manchester managed to build a transmitter covering the city for £6! The most ambitious designs incorporated stereo (for VHF) and live link-ups to a studio. Programming for the new wave of pirates followed the '60s pattern of playing records. Their music was usually of 'minority interest', played by d.j.s who were enthusiasts for a particular style. Jazz-funk provided the inspiration for Radios Horizon, JFM, Invicta and most of London's pirates. Dread Broadcasting Corporation plays reggae and other styles of black music. Radio Phoenix caters for the New Wave audience. *Time Out* once identified 23 different pirates operating in London (Salewicz). So successful has been their action that the Home Office is believed to be moving toward some kind of legalisation (Brooks). A similar operation in television is restricted by the price of transmitters, though Radio Zodiac was offered one for £50. However, cable television and cheapening technology could change this.

● The foreign example of deregulation and community radio. 'When Los Angeles can support more than 20 radio stations, and the Greater Paris area 54 stations, the argument that the current system is the only way forward for allocating broadcasting frequencies appears suspect' (Adam Smith Institute, p. 44). The American example has been used to support the development of a cable television system in Britain (Veljanovski and Bishop). Foreign broadcasting systems furnish the evidence for deregulation and commercial development. Also there exist abroad community radio and television services. Community radio stations exist under very different socio-economic systems, e.g. France, Italy, USA, Yugoslavia and Australia. They more or less conform to the model of a co-operatively run, access station. In France, the stations tend to cater for one particular special interest group, such as Radio Juive, Frequencie Gaie or Radio Soleil (immigrants). In Italy, many of the earliest stations were operated by ultra-leftist political groups, as in Onde Rosse or Radio Alice. In the USA, the stations have acted as umbrella groups for a variety of marginalised groups, as do KPFA and the other Pacifica stations. All of them offer a way of running and programming radio or TV stations not available in Britain.

● The existence of widespread dissatisfaction with the existing services. It is not only the Labour movement that feels the mass media do not meet its interests. Important social groups, such as women, gays and the ethnic minorities feel programming does not cater for their concerns. The GLC Local Radio Forum has received submissions from such groups stating their grievances (GLC). For many of these groups, reform of the existing services does not go far enough. They want to be able to participate directly in programming. They wish to exercise some control over the broadcasting institutions themselves. This involves freeing such institutions from the control of both state and capital, as far as this is possible. The popularity of pirate radio stations in London serving the Afro-Caribbean, Arabic and Greek communities is practical evidence of this.

The radio broadcasting system represents the 'weak link' in the contemporary situation. The expansion of cable and satellite TV is still a number of years off. The legalisation of new radio stations involves no large capital investment. It is a matter of the Home Office deciding to release the vacant frequencies for legal broadcasting. Therefore, it is vital that the Left understands what is developing. It must learn how to intervene in ways that will both serve the interests of the Labour movement and the working class as a whole.

A Political Economy of the Mass Media?

It is the contention of this article that the work of Karl Marx is still the best starting place for an informed examination of the mass media. But cultural production has presented real problems for many Marxist commentators. Especially when it concerned the provision of broadcasting services, there has been a tendency to see the production of any non-tangible good as part of 'non-productive' labour (e.g. Baran). By placing cultural production in the ideological and political superstructure of bourgeois society, it is divorced from the economic base. Lenin is primarily concerned with the political effects of the newspaper. The ideological position of the mass media has been the central concern of most

Leninists, from Althusserians to Trotskyists. But Marx's major work centred on the study and critique of political economy. Given the inability of the present analyses to give a credible response, perhaps it would be useful to utilise Marx's work on capitalism as a mode of production. Marx saw that the characteristics of capitalist production do not lie in *what* is produced. Instead he looked at the social forms which govern human labour.

> A singer who sings like a bird is an unproductive worker. But if she sells her song for money, she is to that extent a wage-labourer or merchant. But if the same singer is engaged by an entrepreneur who makes her sing to make money, then she becomes a productive worker, since she *produces* capital directly (Marx, 1976, p. 1044).

This makes the view that the economic base is only 'determinant in the last instance' very doubtful. Instead an analysis of the mass media should start with the Marxian categories of commodity, money, wage labour, capital accumulation, etc. This can be seen clearly in the music business. A record company invests its money in both fixed capital (recording studios, pressing plants, etc.) and variable capital (the living labour of musicians, engineers and factory workers) to produce a veritable commodity: a record. This can be sold to valorise the commodity, so bringing about capital accumulation. The problem for the nascent radio broadcasting industry was to sell its programmes to the owners of wireless sets in the same way as records are to gramophone owners. The difficulty lay in the material-technical basis of the industry. It propagated its programming through the electro-magnetic spectrum. But once the radio set had been purchased, the reception of signals was free. Today, scrambled signals and rented decoders could enforce sale at the moment of consumption. In the 1920s, when radio broadcasting began, no such solution was feasible. In a capitalist mode of production, the problem of how to valorise capital is of central importance. Both private and state ownership provided different solutions to the obstacles to commoditising radio broadcasting.

In the USA, the selling of airtime to advertisers turned the output of a radio station into a commodity. The main purchasers were corporations who wanted to peddle their wares to the listening public. The radio stations competed to maximise their audiences to gain more advertising revenue. This form of commoditisation allowed radio stations to remain in the hands of private capitalists. Other groups, notably fundamentalist Christian and right-wing political sects, purchased both airtime and stations. When commercial broadcasting arrived in Britain, it too was financed by the selling of airtime for advertisements. But Britain had pioneered a different solution to overcoming the material-technical limitations of broadcasting to valorisation. This was the compulsory sale of programming. The listener is forced to pay a licence fee on the wireless set. Though it appears as a form of regressive taxation, the licence fee directly finances the operations of the BBC. It was this reliance on state intervention to fund itself that made the BBC into a public corporation.

When it is stated that there is 'a battle between the public service and market modes of cultural production and consumption' (Garnham, p. 20), a certain amount of scepticism is necessary. Is there such a dramatic difference between the statised and commercial broadcasting services? Some argue that state-owned broadcasting systems are inherently superior:

> . . . its [public regulation of broadcasting] *justification* lies in its superiority to the market as a means of providing all citizens, whatever their wealth or geographical location, equal access to a wide range of high quality entertainment, information and education, and as a means of ensuring that the aim of the programme producer is the satisfaction of a range of audience taste rather than only those tastes that show the largest profit (Garnham, pp. 13-14).

It would be overly reductionist to see *no* distinction between the forms of radio broadcasting thrown up by different, historically specific manifestations of bourgeois social relations. There are marked divergences in output between services based on selling advertising and one financed through a licence fee. But it is equally blind not to see the close similarities that exist between state and private broadcasting institutions: '. . . the BBC is already heavily commercialised. It competes with independent television [and radio] for audiences in a quite unrestrained manner; and it devotes much air-time to advertising its own products – books, computers, records, videos, etc.' (Adam Smith Institute, p. 39).

It also competes against other types of entertainment: books, theatre, sports and records. But, for Garnham and those like him, the distinction is based on their political position. Ideologically, they still inhabit the world of *Iskra*. Economically, they live in the state-financed world of the BBC, university and local government. Fabianism and Bolshevism can unite in defence of the BBC! Both agree that any nationalised industry must be inherently non-capitalist and the representative of a superior mode of production. But is the Left being mobilised simply to defend the state capitalist wing of the 'mixed economy' against its corporate rivals? Do state capitalist institutions represent the threshold of Socialism (as in Lenin, 1963)? A number of questions must be asked.

● How far has public sector broadcasting broken with capitalist social relations of production? The BBC is organised as a classic capitalist labour process. As in other spheres of production, the workforce's relationship with the means of production is mediated through *wage labour*. As a professional labour force, the workers in public broadcasting have only· a limited amount of autonomy of decision-making. The BBC has a clear distinction between the engineering, production and management grades. This is organised around a 'scalar chain': the division between mental and manual labour (Braverman; Marx, 1976). This allows the close supervision of the nature and content of the work performed.

● How far do the workforce have·a say in the management of public broadcasting? At the top of the BBC's management structure sits the Board of Governors. They are selected from the 'great and good' – and definitely not the workforce or listeners. Separated from the means of production, the workforce can only fight very ineffectively against internal censorship. The campaign by the broadcasting unions to support the 'right of reply' *could* represent the first step towards some form of workers' control.

● Do the 'public' own the public broadcasting services in any meaningful way? Ever since Lord Reith, the BBC has sought institutional independence from the government. This has shielded the Corporation from direct party patronage, while retaining leadership in the hands of a select group of people (Hood, pp. 39-52). The wider listenership has not been involved. The division of labour separates the workers of the BBC from the rest of society. Participation in radio and television is limited to interviews, vox pops and phone-ins. Access shows are very rare. Education in the use of the technologies of radio and television is not widely available. The mass of the population exist as passive consumers of its output. The BBC is similar to the other state corporations, such as the NCB, BL or British Steel. It is the real dissatisfaction with these in institutions that allowed the Tories to launch their asset-stripping (privatisation) campaign against the public sector.

It should not be surprising that the BBC neither breaks with capitalism as a labour process or exhibits any signs of working class power. It has been part of a general involvement by the state in capitalist production. Wars and slumps have forced an evolving co-operation between the state and private capital (Mattick). Radio broadcasting shows all types of state interventionism. The most elementary form of state regulation is the assigning of frequencies. This secures bourgeois property rights in the radio spectrum. Organisations such as the IBA restrict entry into the marketplace. This protectionism is a common feature of many nascent industries. Guaranteeing a monopoly of selling radio advertising in a particular locality is one way to ensure the survival of commercial stations. Once high profits are made, it is not surprising that other capitalists press for the barriers to be lowered. The substitution of the state for private capital is another way enterprises of doubtful profitability can be secured. So both the BBC and IBA are legacies of the British state guiding and nurturing new production processes. It is their success that has brought pressures to open up broadcasting to more commercial ventures.

Therefore it is ironic that the demands for a 'right of reply', access and accountability have been subsumed within the campaign to defend public service broadcasting. For these demands question the structures of both private and public broadcasting, seeing them as a 'duopoly'. Ultimately they lead to the desire for self-management, not state ownership.

The Campaign for Community Radio in Britain

The alternative to a state broadcasting service is a system of community stations. These would be run co-operatively, would be non-profit-making and would encourage public participation in broadcasting (Partridge). There have been brief experiments with community cable television stations (Lewis). But the skills of radio are easier to teach, radio stations are cheaper and it is here that direct action – radio piracy – is taking place. Therefore demands for community broadcasting have centred around radio. Cheaper video equipment and programme-hungry cable television stations may change this.

The Home Office represents the major obstacle to the development of community radio in Britain. Even before the First World War, the British state declared that it owned the nation's airwaves (Briggs). It used the necessity for the technical regulation of stations (to stop interference) to impose political control over broadcasting. Community radio campaigners are faced with the problem of securing legalisation. The practical problems of running an 'on-air' station can only be tackled as hypotheses. Public support can be appealed to with difficulty, as listeners cannot demand a service most have never heard. Simon Partridge has dubbed this the 'chicken-and-egg' conundrum. Without

Home Office approval, no competent experiments in community radio broadcasting can be attempted.

The nearest Britain came to having community radio services was after the publication of the findings of the Committee on the Future of Broadcasting chaired by Lord Annan. This had been set up by Harold Wilson to stall left-wing critics of the mass media within the Labour Party and trade unions. The Annan Committee recommended the establishment of a Local Broadcasting Authority (LBA). This would have taken over both the IBA and BBC local radio stations. But it would have also encouraged new types of radio stations.

> . . . we want to see the LBA breaking out of the present mould of financing broadcasting, and encouraging the growth of co-operative and other joint forms of financing to stimulate a direct involvement by the community in its own broadcasting services (Annan, p. 209).

The recommendations of the Committee were never translated into reality. Merlyn Rees, the then Home Secretary, succumbed to pressure from the BBC to squash the idea of a LBA. This was despite a suppressed internal report that had advocated that the BBC should support community radio (Pitt and Mansfield). Since the Annan Committee, the idea of community radio has continued to be pressed by various lobby groups. But the Home Office has become mesmerised with a vision of a high-tech future based around cable and satellite television. Even so, the Home Office does occasionally make noises about community radio. The Third Report of the Home Office Local Radio Working Party considered the issue in 1980. It looked at demands for experiments in community broadcasting and concluded:

> While community radio offers some very interesting possibilities, it is not clear to us that it should take priority, when resources are already fully stretched, over [Channel 4, TV-AM, cable and satellite television] developments. Nonetheless, the opportunities for community radio might be followed up at an appropriate time, and we remain of an open mind on this subject (HOLRWP, p. 47).

Considering the Working Party is drawn exclusively from the Home Office, IBA and BBC representatives, it is not surprising that alternative services were considered to be of low importance. Objections to an immediate issue of experimental licences centred around the problem of regulation (pp. 39-45) and the availability of frequencies (pp. 37-39). Neither difficulty is any real obstacle to the establishment of community radio. But it does reveal the close complicity between the State and the broadcasting institutions.

Frequency regulation is the example of a political decision

hiding behind a technical problem. Only one signal can be sent out on one frequency, otherwise interference results. The availability of these frequencies is limited by the extent of the wavebands present on the domestic radio set. Yet their allocation is based on an entirely *social* decision. The Home Office is beholden to the World Administrative Radio Conference (WARC), which regulates broadcasting on an international level. But even within the restricted range of frequencies laid down by WARC, the Home Office *chooses* not to use all of them. This can be most clearly seen in the gaps between stations on a domestic radio set. Despite a ruling from WARC, the Home Office has shown great reluctance to move the police and emergency services from Band II of the VHF spectrum, so releasing it for radio broadcasting. By claiming that there are no vacant frequencies, the Home Office can protect the BBC and IBA duopoly behind a technological smokescreen. Unfortunately for them, other engineers have exposed their band-planning.

> Technically, sound broadcasting in this country, although competently engineered, is in a mess. The v.h.f. band II is sadly neglected by the public and rarely promoted by broadcasters. It is ineffectively used by the BBC for an ugly hotch-potch of services on the national networks; the local stations, given the choice between f.m. and a.m. would choose the latter any day. Radio 2 is wastefully duplicated on literally dozens of unnecessary frequencies for long periods of time, while other services, or *would-be services*, are denied any frequencies at all (McLeod, p. 41, emphasis mine).

The Home Office, under both Labour and Conservative governments, ignored these arguments for as long as community radio was not a political issue. The community radio movement in Britain therefore was formed to raise public awareness. It first emerged from COMCOM (Community Communications), a body formed to lobby the Annan Committee. This consisted of concerned academics and media professionals who saw community radio stations as part of the extension of cultural facilities to the working class under the auspices of welfare capitalism. Groups such as the cable radio stations and London Open Radio lobbied for the granting of experimental licences to them. But they remained small bands of activists.

Only with the advent of pirate radio has the 'chicken-and-egg' problem been partially overcome. Direct action has allowed new services to come into existence temporarily, forcing the Home Office to confront the issue of regulating new stations. Most pirate stations have little relationship with the community radio movement. To some, it is nothing more than a slogan, describing

OUR RADIO

BM box 103 fm, London WC1

9 out of 10 cats prefer OUR RADIO!

Our Radio is an open access Community Radio Station,at present illegal.It began in February 1982 and has been gradually expanded,giving a regular service.
At present we are transmitting with Dread Broadcasting Corporation,a black reggae evening, on Fridays,10.00pm to 2.00pm,and a whole evening of alternative entertainment on Wednesdays.
In the near future Our Radio will be expanding ,we hope eventually to go out 7 nights a week,and due to the brilliance of our transmitter design you can pick us up loud and clear in most areas of London.
At present Our Radio has no income at all,so any and all donations are welcome..But most of all we need your ideas, tapes,groups willing to make regular programmes or items, as well as any spare sound equipment,records,and publicity. It would be easier to say that we need EVERYTHING.

The schedule for Wednesday evenings is this at present:

5.00 to 6.00pm. Radio Solidarity
News views and music from 'occupied' Poland. Half of the programme is in Polish,and it has a wide audience among London's Polish minority.
6.00 to 7.00pm. Women on the Waves.
A programme by women for women. Recent programmes have had features on Greenham Womens Peace Camp and the demo by the English Collective of Prostitutes. Great music too,all women.
7.00 to 9.00pm. Gaywaves.
Britain's first homosexual wireless programme. News,whats on,music,and various outrageous events.Is looking for more gay groups to do 15 minute time slots.Stars Anvil Chime and Zaphod McBeeblebrok.
9.00 to 10.00pm. The Message
Radical radio at its best.Includes mad take offs,wild attacks interviews, squatting news and all the information you want to hear but the straight media filters out.Plus music to fit.
10.00 to 11.00pm. Utapia.
Utapia is an independent cassette radio show. Music you definitely wont hear anywhere else,none of it on record, all of it lively.
11.00 till Late. THE BAG.
The notorious BAG is a programme of music and cut ups, but without that nagging DJ to bother you. Each programme is based around a theme..Religion/Money/Society..The Under Cover BAG Operation.The Good,the BAG and the Ugly..etc.

~"open access community Radio Station"~

more the limited range of their transmitters than anything else. The clandestine nature of their broadcasts precluded any formal links between a station and its audience. One pirate station, Dread Broadcasting Corporation (DBC), does see itself as more than just a music station. It wishes to set up a London-wide station catering for the Afro-Caribbean community. However, none of the pirates followed the example of Radio Free Derry, which had been an overtly political station (McCann, pp. 53-54). This is because most pirates operate self-censorship. The broadcasting of controversial material leads to rapid Home Office action.

OUR RADIO, a pirate station in London, was foolhardy enough to try to break these conventions. This station deliberately tried to set up a community radio-style service. It was a collection of disparate groups coming together to broadcast their material. Programmes were made by Polish exiles, feminists, gays, squatters and radical d.j.s (See Table 1). For over a year it operated with little harassment from the Home Office, with its major difficulties being its own disorganisation and lack of money. But between February and March 1983, its Wednesday night transmissions were subject to weekly raids until it was forced off the air. In court, one supporter was fined £200, plus £100 costs, for his participation in what the Home Office described as a 'homosexual and anarchist/terrorist' station! Though it collapsed under external and internal pressures, OUR RADIO remains London's only attempt at an 'on-air' community radio station. It left a reputation better than its actual programming!

Sheffield Peace Radio followed OUR RADIO's model for a

DENNIS BARKER reports on the pirates who tune in to Radio Trent

Voice of Arthur blights the air

POLITICAL pirate radio, a rarity in Britain, is rearing its head again. It has nudged its way into the coalminers' strike on the side of Arthur Scargill.

It is the first recorded instance of a pirate radio station broadcasting political material since Radio Enoch stopped its racial broadcasts when British Telecom investigators got close. That was at the beginning of last year.

The pro-Scargill pirate radio is causing the Department of Trade and Industry (which has now absorbed the investigative side of British Telecom prior to its privatisation) even more trouble, because it is probably being operated from a series of private houses or a car boot.

The denunciations of "scabs" and the "geriatric axeman Ian MacGregor" have been going out in the Nottingham area on the same medium wave frequency (301) as Radio Trent in Nottingham. Earlier this week the transmissions worried Radio Trent even more by also going out on VHF frequencies.

"It is a sinister development, because it may mean the pirates have found some way of getting in to the Independent Local Radio System," said Mr Ron Coles, managing director of Radio Trent.

For the past six weeks pro-Scargill Pirate Radio has

been on air only spasmodically, exactly at the same time as Radio Trent news bulletins. Mr Coles said that he was not suggesting that Mr Scargill personally was broadcasting, but extracts from his speeches could have been taped from radio, television or live meetings.

Mr Coles has been inundated with telephone calls from angry listeners, especially housewives who think that it is Radio Trent itself which has been broadcasting the exhortations of Mr Scargill against a background of martial music or Parry's Jerusalem.

"Either they think it is us and are angry, or they know it is not us, but think we are doing nothing to stop it," said Mr Coles. "But it is difficult to stop because it is difficult to trace the broadcasts because they are so spasmodic and seem to be made from different places."

Radio Trent has complained to the Independent Broadcasting Authority, the Home Office and the DTI. Unfortunately the DTI is short of staff in the Nottingham area which has cut down investigations.

Mr Coles would not say how the pirates might have "penetrated the system" of ILR broadcasting itself to put out its newer VHF broadcasts. "I don't want to help other people do it," he said. "Things are bad enough as they are."

Guardian, 22 August 1984

few months, only to be shut down by the police after intensive surveillance. The station was told that the word 'Peace' in their name had attracted special attention from the state. During the 1984 miners' strike, Radio Trent's news broadcasts were interrupted by a pro-strike pirate station, 'The Voice of Arthur', using a level of technological sophistication unmatched by other stations.

The anarchists involved in pirate radio have seen illegality as an end in itself. Only as a pirate is a station free of capitalist control, they believe. but the material-technical basis of radio broadcasting militates against this: a radio transmitter broadcasts from one point to many receivers, so it is very easy for the police and Home Office to track down pirate stations. OUR RADIO learned this the hard way. (Even with the backing of the Polish proletariat, Radio Solidarnose can only stay transmitting for five or ten minutes before the Zomo arrive.) On the other hand, the British state's general tolerance of pirate radio stations can be interpreted as a sign of imminent legalisation. Therefore, it is necessary for both legal lobbying and direct action to be linked together. The problem is not to avoid state regulation, but for legalisation to take the form where the possibilities of community radio can be realised.

Is Community Radio Non-Capitalist?

In July 1984 the new Telecommunications Bill came into operation. This closed a loophole which had allowed a number of pirate radio stations to transmit in London full-time. The Home Office is following a policy of *criminalisation* by turning illegal broadcasting from a minor misdemeanour to a serious offence. This may reduce the pirates to ship-born operations or short guerrilla transmissions, though enforcement so far has been patchy. Therefore the Left has a vital interest in the shape of any legal radio stations that may emerge.

The radical nature of community broadcasting does not lie in an openly agitational role. For example, after years of conflict with the authorities, Radio Alice in Bologna was finally shut down while broadcasting phone calls from workers and students taking part in an uprising there (Red Notes, pp. 31-32). The impracticability of using expensive, fixed-point transmitters in an uprising is shown by this example. The rioters in Britain in the summer of 1981 used the less vulnerable and more portable C.B. radios for their communications.

Community radio's use lies elsewhere. It is not some electronic *Iskra*, calling the masses to battle. Nor is it the platform for an elite group of intellectuals to put forward their claim to revolutionary leadership. It is not even a facility for a closed circle of professional journalists, however 'ideologically sound', to mediate between listeners and social events. Rather, what is subversive about community radio is the way it can challenge the division between broadcasters and consumers in our society. A community radio station seeks to adopt an organisational form which allows a wide variety of people to broadcast – i.e., it can attempt to transcend the capitalist labour process. Their perceptions and views might well not be the 'truth' (pravda!), but it is their opinion.

The radio station should educate its listeners so that they can themselves become contributors to programming. The ability to make specialist programming will provide a focus for and contact within ethnic, cultural or political groups. As they are broadcast, cross-communication can happen between different cultures and outlooks. A station based around one neighbourhood, or appealing to a particular community, can become a noticeboard receiving contributions from (at least potentially) the whole listenership. The radio station can interact with other forms of communication, such as the telephone, C.B. radio, home computers, etc. There are many unforeseen potentialities for using community radio (Barbrook and Knight, pp. 16-17). The Left should look at the example of Radio Donna in Rome. This women's station did not lecture its audience in feminist politics. Instead, it sought to break down the isolation of women trapped at home. Radicalisation occurred through participation in the programming.

This is why the Left can take advantage of any loosening of state control over the radio spectrum. The Home Office is considering the legalisation of new stations by 1990. The defence of the status quo, or even of an idealised version of public service broadcasting, provides no real response to this challenge. Resistance to change is likely to be swept away by the demands of listeners for new services, even if commercially provided, and the dreams of entrepreneurs of easy profits.

Community radio can provide the only response by the Left. In bourgeois society, the word 'community' has many meanings. It can represent the humane face of capitalism, seeking to defuse tensions rather than cause confrontation. It is used in this fashion to describe community policemen! On the other hand, it can signify the control of a local neighbourhood or ethnic/cultural group over its own social space. By basing its practice around the struggle for self-management, this concept of community harks back to the original meaning of *communism*.

In this way, community radio stations link up with the rise of the libertarian Left in the 1960s. KPFA in Berkeley was turned into a workers' cooperative by members who were active in the Anti-Vietnam war movement. In Italy, community radio stations emerged directly from left-wing groups engaged in a theoretical and practical critique of the Italian Communist Party (Pond and Ordonez; Red Notes, pp. 33-35). The British community radio movement is part of a general flourishing of grassroots organisations: housing co-ops, arts labs, worker co-ops, etc. This 'counter-culture' has seen itself as challenging not only capitalist methods, but also the bureaucratic statism embraced by both the reformist and revolutionary wings of Socialism. Community radio represents the extension of these ideas of democratic self-management and skill-sharing into radio broadcasting.

These forms of organisation can be said to prefigure socialism in their structure. However this does not mean they are self-sufficient and autonomous bodies ('Socialism in one radio station'). Rather, they are limited by the workings of both the state and the market. No organisation can be entirely free of value relations in bourgeois society. A community radio station will have to carry out that essence of capitalism, balancing the books. To survive, it will have to sell advertising, raise subscriptions from its listeners and/or rely on government grants. To ensure that the station maintains a continuous service, there will be a nucleus of professional workers. The division of labour between administration, engineers and programmers will be only partially overcome. Even its programming will have to be tailored to ensure that the station can raise the money to break even. The state will maintain a role in radio broadcasting. The need to assign frequencies gives the state a power over radio which it lost over the press in the nineteenth century. Output of a community radio station will be checked not only by fear of losing a licence. The laws of slander, libel, Official Secrets and sedition provide a host of legal restrictions.

The struggle of community radio stations to stop themselves succumbing to financial and legal pressures can inform the theoretical understanding of the Left. It is a practice that could clear some of the confusions touched on above. The community radio movement can centre the debate on *who* owns and controls the mass media. Co-operative organisation must be seen as the substitute for both commercial and state capitalism. The technological restructuring of the mass media should not be feared if this can be the opportunity for extending forms of self-management. Above all, state censorship should be resisted in favour of democratic structures within broadcasting. This seems to make the community radio movement a challenge to the established practices of both the Labour Party and the trade unions. The hostility of the Campaign for Press and Broadcasting Freedom to community radio seems to confirm this. Yet the tradition of bureaucratic statism in both sections of the Labour movement has been subject to radical criticism. Both the 'hard left' of the Labour Party and those groups such as the Lucas Aerospace Shop Stewards Combine extend the demands for accountability and control into the party and unions.

It should therefore not be surprising that the GLC is intervening to help the community radio movement. One of the most successful (or infamous) policies of the GLC has been the funding of various community and voluntary groups (Carvel, pp. 206-11). John McDonnell, the Chair of Finance and General Purposes, has been instrumental in setting up a Local Radio Forum to examine London's radio services. Out of its deliberations should come funding for various community radio projects in London. These could provide the studios and social base for groups wishing to take advantage of any relaxation in the Home Office's attitudes. The GLC's role should not be seen simply as the provider of money. The Labour movement's interest in more democratic forms of broadcasting lies beyond the hope of getting more sympathetic coverage. Within the Labour Left, there is an awareness of the need to create a new vision of Socialism. The rediscovery of the possibilities of co-operative solutions to transcend capitalist social relations is part of this process. For example, Tony Benn has stated that the Labour Party must be the representative of the working class in all its diverse forms of self-organisation (Benn, 1984).

The community radio movement is drawn into this struggle. Legalisation does not remove the limitations placed on broadcasting by the market and the state. But the democratisation of part of the mass media is an important reform. It can play a decisive role in the fight for political power. It can be an integral part of the general transformation of bourgeois society.

Therefore it can be seen that community radio poses many questions, challenging the British Left's long-held preconceptions about the mass media. But it also offers a practice which could resolve these difficulties – and in areas other than just radio. Support for initiatives such as community radio shows a way that the Left can positively intervene into the debate about the future of broadcasting. Not only would this pre-empt the Tories' appeal of provision by commercial companies; it could even provide us with some interesting, innovative and exciting radio stations!

It is contrary to history to represent work for reforms as a long-drawn-out revolution and revolution as a condensed series of reforms. A social transformation and a legislative reform do not differ according to their duration but according to their content. The secret of historic change through the utilisation of political power resides precisely in the transformation of simple quantitative modification into a new quality, or to speak more concretely, in the passage of a historic period from one given form of society to another (Luxembourg, p. 77).

Bibliography

Thanks to Simon Partridge, Simon Schaffer, Peter Bevington, the Radical Science Collective and David McLellan's lentil seminar group.

The Community Radio Association can be contacted at 92 Huddleston Road, London N7 0EG. Tel. 01-263-6692.

Adam Smith Institute. *Omega Report: Communications Policy*, ASI, 1984.

Lord Annan, *Report of the Committee on the Future of Broadcasting*, HMSO, 1977.

Paul Baran, *The Political Economy of Growth*, Pelican, 1973.

Richard Barbrook and Chris Knight, 'A "Briefing" on the Airwaves', *London Labour Briefing* 31 (July 1983).

Tony Benn, Column in *Guardian*, 19 December 1983.

. 'Labour's Alliance for Socialism', *Socialist Action* 56 (4 May 1984).

Harry Braverman, *Labor and Monopoly Capital*, Monthly Review Press, 1974.

Asa Briggs, *The History of Broadcasting in the United Kingdom*, Oxford, OUP, 1961.

Richard Brooks, 'All-clear for Radio Pirates', *Sunday Times*, 20 May 1984.

Campaign for Free Speech on Ireland, *The British Media and Ireland – Truth: the First Casualty*, CFSI, undated.

Campaign for Press Freedom, *Towards Press Freedom*, CPF, 1979.

. *The Right of Reply*, CPF, 1981.

Campaign for Press and Broadcasting Freedom, *Press, Radio and Television*, Comedia, 1983.

John Carvel, *Citizen Ken*, Chatto and Windus, London, 1984.

Daniel and Gabriel Cohn-Bendit, *Obsolete Communism: The Left-Wing Alternative*, Penguin, 1969.

Ian Connell, 'Commercial Broadcasting and the British Left', *Screen, 24*, 6 (Nov-Dec 1983).

Chris Cooper, 'Free Market Broadcasting', *Political Notes 9*, Libertarian Alliance, 1983.
CSE Communications Group, *Hunt on Cable TV: Chaos or Coherence?* CPBF, 1982.
Nicholas Garnham, 'Public Service versus the Market', *Screen, 24*, 1 (Jan-Feb 1983).
Glasgow University Media Group, *Bad News*, RKP, 1976.
Greater London Council, *Strategy for the Development of Local Radio in London*, GLC, 1983.
Andrew Goodman, 'Workshop for Television – the Experience of Censorship and Control', in Paul Beharrell and Greg Philo, *Trade Unions and the Media*, Macmillan, 1977.
Stuart Hall, Chas Critcher, Tony Jefferson, John Clarke, Brian Roberts, *Policing the Crisis*, Macmillan, 1978.
Caroline Heller, *Broadcasting and Accountability*, BFI, 1978.
Home Office Local Radio Working Party, *Third Report*, Home Office, 1980.
Stuart Hood, *On Television*, Pluto, 1980.
Labour Party, *New Hope for Britain*, Labour Party, 1983.
Vladimir Lenin, "Left-Wing" Childishness and the Petty-Bourgeois Mentality in *Selected Works*, Vol 2, Progress,Moscow, 1963.
, *What is to be Done?*, Peking, Foreign Languages Press, 1975.
, *Imperialism: the Highest Stage of Capitalism*, Progress, Moscow, 1978.
, 'Party Organisation and Party Literature', in Maynard Solomon, *Marxism and Art*, Harvester Press, 1979.
Peter Lewis, *Bristol Channel and Community Television*, IBA, 1976.
Local Radio Workshop, *Local Radio in London*, LRW, 1982.
, *Capital: Local Radio and Private Profit*, Comedia, 1983.
Rosa Luxemburg, *Rosa Luxemburg Speaks*, NY, Pathfinder, 1970.
Karl Marx and Friedrich Engels, *Manifesto of the Communist Party*, Peking, Foreign Languages Press, 1975.
, *The German Ideology*, Lawrence and Wishart, 1977.
Karl Marx, *Capital*, Vol 1, Penguin, 1976.
Eamonn McCann, *War and an Irish Town*, Penguin, 1974.
Norman McLeod, 'Community Radio: a Case for More Accessible Local Broadcasting', in *Wireless World*, June/July 1980.
Paul Mattick, *Marx and Keynes: the Limits of the Mixed Economy*, Merlin, 1973.
Graham Murdock and Peter Goulding, 'Beyond Monopoly – Mass Communications in the Age of Conglomerates', in Peter Beharrell and Greg Philo, *Trade Unions and the Media*, Macmillan, 1977.
Simon Partridge, *Not the BBC/IBA: the Case for Community Radio*, Comedia, 1982.
Tim Pitt and Frank Mansfield, *London Community Radio Study*, BBC, 1978 (suppressed).

Alan Pond and Carlos Ordonez, 'Italian Radio Lessons', in *Relay*, 3, Summer 1983.

Red Notes, *Italy 1977-8: Living with an Earthquake*, Red Notes, 1978.

Geoffrey Robertson, 'Chain-Saw Censor', *Guardian*, 14 March 1984.

Chris Salewicz, 'Rebel Radios', *Time Out*, 606, 2-8 April 1982, 14-17.

Denis Thomas, *Competition in Radio*, Institute of Economic Affairs, Occasional Papers 5, 1965.

C.G. Veljanovski and W.D. Bishop, *Choice by Cable: The Economics of a New Era in Television*, Institute of Economic Affairs, Hobart Paper 96, 1983.

PUBLIC ACCESS TELEVISION: ALTERNATIVE VIEWS

Douglas Kellner

A community will evolve only when a people control their own communications.

Frantz Fanon

In *1984* George Orwell projected a view of the future in which the mass media were a prime vehicle of social control and political indoctrination. The American and European Left have followed Orwell in seeing capitalist and state-capitalist controlled media as instruments of manipulation and, with some notable exceptions, have regularly denounced the media as tools of ruling class domination and social control. In Germany, for example, the Frankfurt school regularly criticized the media for promoting bourgeois ideology and debasing culture, and – unlike Brecht, Benjamin, and Enzensberger – rarely considered media like radio, film, or television as potential instruments of liberation (Kellner, 1982). The New Left and counterculture, too, in the United States tended to perceive the media as instruments of capitalist manipulation, although, as Todd Gitlin has argued, much New Left politics was (and continues to be) aimed at the media, which was perceived as a means of gaining access to the public (Gitlin).

Political activity geared toward the dominant media takes the risk, of course, that it will be distorted or fragmented by media presentation. In addition, it seems questionable to spend weeks organizing demonstrations, press conferences, or events that, if at all, are presented in 30-second clips on a television news program, or are given a few lines play in a newspaper story. However, public access television, I shall argue, presents quite another possibility for the Left to meaningfully use the broadcast media to transmit alternative information, to legitimate progressive struggles and social movements, and to attempt to shape public opinion and use the media as instruments of political intervention.

Dan Thibidoux

Big Brother, We're Watching

The Left, Broadcast Media and Technology

But first the Left must overcome its biases against technology and the media, especially television. There has been a long tradition of technophobia on the Left, just as there has been a long tradition fetishizing science and technology. And the mass media have been seen by many on the Left, including Leninists who usually are positive toward technology, as particularly potent instruments of manipulation and social control in the hands of the ruling class. Broadcast media, especially television, have been especially subject to denunciation and dismissal, and one US counter-cultural book seriously proposed *Four Arguments for the Elimination of Television* (Mander).

Part of the problem is that the Left has been excessively oriented toward print media; it thinks that publishing journals, newspapers and handouts constitutes the highest form of political communication. Certainly, Left print media are an important part of developing an oppositional public sphere, but it is often at the expense of neglecting other forms of political communication, especially broadcast media (Habermas; Negt-Kluge). Although suspicion and a critical posture toward broadcast media are certainly justified, it is self-defeating simply to denounce television, for example, as an instrument of bourgeois hegemony *tout court*. For in fact, television and broadcast media stand at the center of everyday life and are crucial instruments of politics and public opinion. If the Left surrenders these powerful instruments of communication to the Right and to the ruling classes, then we are excluding ourselves from an important field of political and cultural struggle. Instead the Left should develop a radical media politics, including strategies to use broadcast media.

Previously, there was little possibility for the Left to make use of the broadcast media in the capitalist countries. Commercially-owned and controlled television in the United States and state-controlled television in Europe traditionally have utilized the media as instruments of corporate and state power (Barnouw; Briggs; Mattelart-Siegellaub, 1979). The history of broadcast media in the United States shows corporate control intervening at key junctures in broadcast history to eliminate possibilities of more democratic use of the broadcast media which would make possible a broader range of viewpoints and types of programming (Mosco).[1] Consequently, socialist and other oppositional groups have been effectively denied access to broadcast media and thus have been effectively excluded from mainstream political debate in an era in which public communication has been dominated by broadcast media.

In the United States, the advent of cable and satellite television has modified this situation somewhat.[2] Expanding cable systems have required new material; there have been several news networks, many more discussion programs, uncut films, more documentaries, and networks evolving devoted to black, hispanic, women, religious, business, labor, and other interest-group programming. Network hegemony of broadcasting is thus eroding but has hardly disappeared, despite the appearance of a greater diversity of programming since the 1970s (Kellner, 1979, 1981). And these new cable networks have not yet opened themselves to radical documentary, film or discussion shows. So, for the Left, the development of pirate radio and public access television are the most promising developments within the new communication media. Throughout Europe, and less so in the US, use has been made of radio stations, controlled and operated by Leftists, to broadcast progressive political communication and points of view – news, information, music and entertainment, discussion (Mattelart-Siegellaub, 1983). In the United States, the existence of public access television, in some places operative since the early 1970s, also gives the Left access to broadcast media in which we can make our own programs and control their content. Since cable and public access are rapidly proliferating throughout the United States,[3] and have just begun in Europe, I wish to provide some information on the US experience and make some strategic proposals based on a project that I have been involved in here in Austin, Texas since 1978.

Public Access Television: The US Experience

When cable television began to be widely introduced in the early 1970s, the Federal Communication Commission mandated in 1972 that 'beginning in 1972, new cable systems (and after 1977, all cable systems) in the 100 largest television markets be required to provide channels for government, for educational purposes, and most importantly, for public access' (Shapiro). This suggested, in fact, that cable systems should make available three public access channels for state and local government, education and community public access use. 'Public access' was construed to mean that the cable company should make available equipment and air-time so that literally anybody could make use of the access channel and say and do anything that they wished on a first-come, first-served basis, subject only to obscenity and libel laws. Managing the access channel required, in most cases, setting up a local organization to manage the access system.

In the beginning, however, few, if any, cable systems made as many as three channels available, though some systems began offering one or two access channels in the early to mid-1970s. For the most part, the availability of access channels depended on the political clout of local government and committed (and often unpaid) local groups to convince the cable company, almost all privately owned, to make available an access channel. Here in Austin, for example, a small group of video activists formed Austin Community Television in 1970 and began broadcasting with their own equipment through the cable system that year. Eventually they raised grants to support their activities, buy equipment and pay regular employees salaries. A new cable contract signed in the early 1980s called for the cable company to provide $500,000 a year for access; after a difficult political struggle, which I shall mention later, Austin Community Television was able to get at least $300,000 a year to support their activities. However, this money went for studio, equipment and administrative expenses, so that producers have to raise their own money – though some access systems do pay producers and there are frequently debates as to whether access money should go directly to producers and, if so, how much.

A 1979 Supreme Court decision, however, struck down the 1972 ruling which mandated access, on the grounds that the FCC didn't have the authority to mandate access, an authority which supposedly belongs to the US Congress (Koeing). However, cable was expanding so rapidly and becoming such a high-growth competitive industry that city governments considering cable systems were besieged by companies making lucrative offers (20 to 80 channel cable systems) and were able to negotiate access channels and financial support for a public access system. Consequently, public access grew significantly during the early 1980s.

Where there are operative public access systems, the Left has promising – though not sufficiently explored – possibilities to produce and broadcast their own television programs. Here in Austin, for example, there is now a weekly anti-nuclear program, black and Chicano programs, gay programs, countercultural and anarchist programs, an atheist program, occasional feminist programs and a weekly Left news magazine, *Alternative Views* which has produced over 240 hour-long programs from 1978 to the present on a wide variety of topics. Two surveys, one undertaken by the University of Texas and another commissioned by the cable company, indicate that from 10,000 to 30,000 Austin viewers watch at least one public access television program every night. And national surveys of viewer preferences for cable programs indicate that public access is a high priority for many viewers (ELRA). Thus there is definitely a receptive and growing audience for public access television. The possibility of making alternative television programs by the Left should be a much higher priority for radical media politics.

The program that I've been involved with, *Alternative Views*, has gained a national reputation and a large and loyal audience. We began in 1978 with no television experience and no resources, but we immediately began producing a weekly program, using video equipment and tapes at the University of Texas, and the broadcast and editing facilities of Austin Community Television. In fact, a group wishing to make access programming need have only minimal technical experience or even financial resources to begin producing public access television where there is an access system in place that will make available equipment, technical personnel and video-tapes. Some systems charge money for use of facilities, or charge a fee for use of air-time. But, because of competitive bidding between cable systems in the 1980s for the most lucrative franchises, many cable systems offer free use of equipment, personnel and air-time. In these situations, radicals can make use of public access facilities without technical expertise, television experience or financial resources.

Many access systems also offer training programs concerning how to use the media if a group or individual wants to make their own programs from conception through final editing. And the costs of equipment have been rapidly declining so that it is possible for some groups to even purchase their own video equipment. For the first two years the *Alternative Views* group literally made the program on a zero budget, using University of Texas and Austin Community Television tapes and equipment. From the third year through the fifth year, we raised around $2,000 a year through fund-raisers and appeals to friends so that we could purchase and own our own tapes. In 1984, we received two grants of about $2,000 each and are now making copies available to public access systems in San Antonio, Dallas, Pittsburgh, Urbana and Atlanta. This project, which just began in Spring 1984, will provide a starting point for a left public access network in the US where progressive groups can send their programs to other access systems and begin exchanging tapes.

Eventually, we wish to own our own equipment, but for now we are able to make a weekly program using equipment available to the community. Thus progressive groups can often make use now of video equipment belonging to sympathetic groups or institutions, or access facility equipment, and can produce video programs for public access television and other projects on a very low budget. Indeed, raising money to buy tapes often requires far less money than many print media projects. Consequently, the costs of producing video tapes for public access are not necessarily prohibitive, and groups who want to explore the possibilities of public access television should explore the availability of equipment in their area, or the costs of buying their own tapes and equipment.

From the beginning we were convinced that, despite no previous television experience, we were making programs that were of interest to the community and that we were gaining an appreciative audience. On our first program in October 1978 we had an Iranian student as guest who discussed opposition to the Shah and the possibility of his overthrow; we also had a detailed discussion of the Sandinista movement struggling to overthrow Somoza – weeks before the national broadcast media discovered these movements. We then had two programs on nuclear energy and energy alternatives – topics that later became central for the US Left – with, among other guests, Austinite Ray Reece, whose book *The Sun Betrayed* (South End Press, 1980) later became a definitive text on corporate control and suppression of solar energy. On early shows we also had long interviews with former Senator Ralph Yarborough, a Texas progressive responsible for much legislation, like the national Defense-Education Act, and learned that he had never been interviewed before in depth for television. We also had an electrifying two-hour, two-part interview with former CIA official John Stockwell. He told how he had been drafted into the CIA at the University of Texas, and then discussed CIA recruitment, indoctrination, activities and his own experiences in Africa, Vietnam and then Angola. Stockwell discussed at length why he decided to quit the CIA and write his book, *In Search of Enemies*, which exposed the Angola operation which he had been in charge of. He then went into a long history of CIA abuses and his arguments for why he thought that the CIA should be shut down and a new intelligence service developed.

We got tremendously positive responses for our show and began regularly taping interviews with people who visited Austin as well as with local activists involved in various struggles. The audience included people from every class, ethnic group and strata from the city; we now have a large support group which contributes money and other material aid to the program and a constantly growing audience. As our project developed, we began varying our format using documentary films, slide shows, raw video footage and other visual material to enhance the visual aspect of our program. We also do frequent news sections where we present information – from the left, business, and other print sources – that is not generally presented in mainstream media. In addition, one of our members, Frank Morrow, became skilled at editing and developed some impressive montages of documentary and interview material to illustrate the topics being discussed.

Once the project is underway, there is no problem finding topics, people or resources. We discovered that anyone we wished to interview was happy to come on our program; after we began gaining recognition, local groups and individuals called us regularly to provide topics, speakers, films or other video material. We encouraged some local groups to make their own weekly shows; a variety of peace, countercultural, gay, anti-nuke, chicano, anti-klan, and other groups have done so. And we have continued to serve as an umbrella organization which has produced programs for over one hundred local groups, using their speakers and film or video materials.

Over the years we have also had hour long interviews with anti-war and anti-nuclear activists like Helen Caldecott, George Wald, Michael Klare, David Dellinger and many representatives of the European Peace Movement; we have had interviews with US New Left activists like David MacReynolds, Stokely Carmichael, Greg Calvert and Dr. Spock; many feminists, gays, union activists, and representatives of over 100 local progressive groups have appeared on our show; and officials from the Soviet Union, Cuba, Nicaragua, Allende's government in Chile, the democratic front in El Salvador and many other Third World countries and revolutionary movements have appeared on our show. In addition, we have shown many documentaries and films which various filmmakers and groups have provided for us, and have made some video documentaries ourselves on a variety of topics. Further, we have received raw video footage of the bombing of Lebanon and aftermath of the massacres at Sabra and Shatilla, of the assassinations of five communist labor organizers by the Ku Klux Klan in Greensboro, North Carolina, and of counter-revolutionary activity in Nicaragua.

Most of this material would not be shown on network television, or would be severely cut and censored. Thus the only real possibility today of having alternative television is through the public access/cable television. Obviously progressive groups who want to carry through access projects need to develop a sustained commitment to radical media politics and explore local possibilities for intervention. We began here with a group of eight; but, since most were graduate students who moved elsewhere or took full-time jobs in the city, only two of us have been active throughout the entire project. In particular, the program has depended on the talents and energies of Frank Morrow, who made the project a full-time endeavor during a period when he was working on his Ph.D. at the School of Communications in the University of Texas. But over the years, we have had many people working with us and now have a support group, Friends of Alternative Views, that regularly contributes money, helps with fundraising and publicity and other projects.[4] The first few years we had some internal conflicts concerning topics, format, organization, etc. but worked through these problems. We have functioned rather smoothly in our internal politics during the last few years. (In my conclusion I will mention the external problems that have emerged, both here in Austin and elsewhere in the United States.)

Public Access Television: Problems and Challenges

Once progressive public access television became more wide-spread and popular here in town, it was, of course, subject to political counter-attacks. The conservative daily newspaper in town, for instance, *The Austin American-Statesman*, published frequent denunciations of public access television to the effect that it was controlled by the 'lunatic' fringe of 'socialists, atheists, and radicals' and was not representative of the community as a whole – a lie, since many conservative church groups, business groups and political groups also make use of access. The allegedly poor technical quality was attacked along with the 'irresponsibility' of many of the programs (in fact, technical quality has been constantly improving). In 1983, these criticisms were repeated in editorials and a long article on Austin Community Television in the more liberal monthly magazines *Texas Monthly* and *Third Coast*. The criticisms became more threatening, since Austin Community Television was applying for a five-year renewal of their contract as access manager; certain local interests were attempting to eliminate ACTV and find another access manager and system controlled by city government and local media interests. After a bitter political struggle, the city cable commission and city council approved the renewal of the Austin Community Television access management. For the time being, our access system remains in the control of the community and open to whoever wants to use it, either on a regular basis or occasional basis.[5]

Other US cities have not been so fortunate. One cable company in San Diego arbitrarily closed down their access system after gaining a long-term renewal of their contract; a company recently bought out the San Antonio cable company and threatened to refuse to honor the terms of the previous contract which mandated several access channels; Warners Communications is threatening to renege on earlier contract obligations, which might threaten public access in this system; many systems have never provided access channels; and some rigidly control the access channels and would probably not permit a program like *Alternative Views* to be broadcast. Many cities do have relatively open access channels, however. Where it is possible, the Left should start using this vehicle of political communication and should start attempting to develop a national public access network where tapes can be exchanged and circulated.

Beginnings in this direction are being discussed among various groups, including our own, which is working on developing a Sunbelt public access network as a prelude to a national network. We began this year sending packages of five tapes to contacts in Dallas and San Antonio, and are negotiating with groups in other cities, who would broadcast our program on a regular weekly basis. If this project works and if we can raise more money, we will begin sending packages of five tapes to access systems in other cities. I would like to conclude, however, with some comments on how the Left might make use of public access television in situations in which there already exists cable television and at least the technical potential for public access.

First, groups must explore the availability of an access channel and approach the people in charge of it. Proposals should be made concerning the type of programming that the group wants to produce. The group must see if equipment, training and tapes are available to use. Many video activists and public access systems are open to Leftist projects – more so, for the most part, than the establishment media. This is, at least, the US experience, as radicals have regularly produced programs in such places as Austin, New Orleans, New York, Madison, Pittsburgh, Appalachia, Montana, etc.[6] If an access system exists, alliances must be made with access and video people and then the projects should be developed.

Next, a group must decide if they wish only to produce occasional programs or develop a regular weekly, bi-weekly or monthly series. We began producing weekly one-hour programs as soon as we got the access channel to agree to broadcast our program, and developed our programming organization, philosophy, and projects as we went on. In some cases, it might, however, be better to have more fully developed projects outlined before one begins. Talk show format is, of course, the easiest to adopt and might make a good beginning, though more imaginative uses of video should be developed as experience and expertise expands. A summary of news published in left publications is also relatively simple to do. One can also make video-cassettes of existing films for broadcast on public access; this is also a good way to begin if the films and duplicating equipment are available. Then, as the project progresses, the group may want to begin developing their own documentaries and to mix documentary, film, and discussion formats, and to edit in titles, slides and other images, to make use of the video format.

Public access television is still in a relatively primitive state here in the US and is, I am told, just beginning in Europe. Despite either the absence of public access or obstacles to its use in some parts of the country, where it exists it provides the one opening in the commercial and state broadcasting system that is at least potentially open for Left intervention. Thus progressive groups and individuals who wish to communicate their ideas and visions to a mass audience should consider how they might use public access television in politically progressive ways. It is defeatist and self-defeating simply to dismiss broadcast media as tools of manipulation and to think that print media are the only tools of communication open to the Left. For most people get their news and information from television, which plays a decisive role in defining political realities, shaping public opinion, and determining what is real and legitimate, and what is not to be taken seriously or is to be viewed negatively.

If the Left wants to play a role in US political life, we must come to terms with the realities of electronic communication and develop strategies to make use of new technologies and possibilities for intervention. Surveys have shown that people take more seriously individuals, groups, and politics that appear on TV, and progressive use of television will thus help progressive movements and struggles gain legitimacy and force in the shifting and contradictory field of US politics. The Right has been making effective use of new technologies and media of communication. For the Left to remain distant from broadcast media, or to contemptuously dismiss television, is a luxury that it can no longer afford. The 1980s confront the Left with both new challenges and dangers. If we want to survive and expand, we must increase our mass base and circulate our struggles to more segments of the population. There are, of course, risks that time and energies spent in other projects may be lost in frustrating media politics; but the risks should be taken if the Left wants to grow during the 1980s and begin to intervene more effectively in the changing technological and political environment of the future.

Notes

The Alternative Information Network has been amassing material concerning radical media politics and progressive use of public access television and other new media of communication for production of a future book on these topics. Readers who have material on these topics, or who would like to correspond with us, can write us: Alternative Information Network, PO Box 7279, Austin, Texas 78712. For proposals in revising this paper, I am grateful to Les Levidow, who read and commented on earlier drafts, and to Judith Burton, Mike Jankowski and Frank Morrow of the Alternative Information Network.

1. Mosco shows how corporate control of broadcasting and of the state obstructed the development of a more democratic and varied communications system in the United States through blocking the development of educational radio and television, through postponing the introduction of FM radio and UHF TV, and through inhibiting development of cable and pay-TV. But, although corporate control of broadcast media remains the primary feature of mass communications systems in the US, some new openings have resulted from technological and economic developments and struggles for more media access. It is these openings, however fragile, that I am proposing that the Left investigate and use.

2. I shall not comment here on the complicated issue of whether European Leftists should support or oppose the introduction of cable television into their countries, since this would involve a different issue altogether (i.e. US cultural imperialism vs. the vicissitudes of national European cultures) which I do not have the information to address. I would suspect, however, that progressives in Britain and Europe are not going to be able to stop the juggernaut of cable and satellite television from radically altering existing broadcast systems; therefore the relevant issue for the Left in these countries is: what use can progressive groups make of the new broadcast systems? Unfortunately, of the surveys by Leftists that I have read of public access and community television in Europe, most tend to be hypercritical and dismissive – before the struggles have even gotten underway and had a chance to develop! A parallel situation occurred in the US where a radical communications group completely dismissed the progressive potential of access television based on a study of a couple of years access productions and struggles in New York; see The Network Project, *CATV: End of a Dream*, Notebook #8 (Summer 1974).

3. A directory of access systems put out by the National Federation of Local Cable Programmers, *The Video Register, 1983-84* claims that there are over 700 access facilities operative in the United States. Some of these systems, however, are limited to a channel which prints time, weather and announcements -of local activities. Thus, it is quite difficult to ascertain how many full-blown access centers are operative; it is clear, however, that the number is growing.

4. Those who wish to contribute tax-exempt donations to this project can

send them to the Alternative Information Network, PO Box 7279, Austin, TX 78712.

5. Struggles like these indicate that the US Left can successfully mobilize coalitions and alliances and be an effective force in local politics. Here in Austin, a 'progressive coalition' has successfully beaten business-oriented candidates in city council elections and has won referendums on community issues in over half of the electoral struggles in the last five years or so – whereas business interests previously completely dominated local politics.

6. It is difficult to get up-to-date information on the state of local access projects. Journals like *Access, The Independent, Alternative Media, Community Television Review* and newsletters like those published by The National Federation of Local Cable Programmers and other local access groups have some material, but it is hard to get an overview. Material is provided, however, in the books and articles listed by Anderson, Frederiksen, Price and Wicklein, Radical Software and Zelmer, which also have suggestions on how to develop grassroots video projects and set up community media centers. A booklet by Evonne Ianacone, *Changing More Than the Channel*, provides 'A Citizens Guide to Forming a Media Access Group', though it does not really focus on how to develop a public access program. The National Federation of Local Cable programmers also provides guides concerning how to produce access television, as do some other sources. We would appreciate receiving copies of such guides, as frequently people write us and ask us for material on how to set up an access center or how to produce an access program; we are forced to refer them to material which might not be up-to-date or directly relevant to their interests.

References

Chuck Anderson, *Video Power*, New York; Praeger, 1975.

David Armstrong, *A Trumpet to Arms: Alternative Media in America*, Boston; Houghton Mifflin, 1981.

Erik Barnouw, *A History of Broadcasting in the United States*, 3 volumes, New York; Oxford University Press, 1966, 1968, 1970).

Bertolt Brecht, 'Radio Theory', translated in *Screen, 20*, 1.

Asa Briggs, *The History of Broadcasting in the United Kingdom*, Oxford; Oxford University Press, 1961, 1965, 1970.

ELRA Group of East Lansing, Michigan; survey compiled in 1982 and discussed in *CableVision*, 26 April, 1982.

Hans-Magnus Enzensberger, *The Consciousness Industry*, New York; Seabury, 1974.

H. Allan Frederiksen, *Community Access Video*, Menlo Park; Nowells Publications, 1972.

Todd Gitlin, *The Whole World's Watching*, Berkeley; University of California Press, 1980.

Jurgen Habermas, *Structurwandel der Offentlichkeit*, Berlin, 1962.

Bob Jacobson, 'Video at the Crossroads', *Jump Cut* (May-June 1974).

Nicholas Johnson, *How to Talk Back to Your Television Set*, Boston: Little, Brown and Company, 1970.

Douglas Kellner, 'TV, Ideology, and Emancipatory Popular Culture', *Socialist Review, 45* (Nov-Dec 1979).

Douglas Kellner, 'Network Television and American Society', *Theory and Society, 10*, 1 (Jan-Feb 1981).

Douglas Kellner, 'Kulturindustrie und Massenkommunikation. Die Kritische Theorie und ihre Folgen', in Wolfgang Bonss and Axel Honneth, eds., *Sozialforschung als Kritik*, Frankfurt: Suhrkamp, 1982, pp. 482-515. An expanded version of this study is forthcoming in *Telos*.

Josh Koeing, 'Court Strikes Down FCC Access Rules', *Community Television Review* (Spring 1979).

Jerry Mander, *Four Arguments for the Elimination of Television*, New York: Morrow, 1978.

Armand Mattelart and Seth Siegellaub, eds., *Communication and Class Struggle: 1. Capitalism, Imperialism*, Paris: International General, 1979.

Armand Mattelart and Seth Siegellaub, *Communication and Class Struggle: 2. Liberation, Socialism*, Paris: International General, 1983.

Vincent Mosco, *Broadcasting in the United States*, Norwood, NJ: Ablex, 1979.

Oskar Negt and Alexander Kluge, *Offentlichkeit und Erfahrung. Zur Organisationsanalyse von burgerlicher und proletarischer Offentlichkeit*, Frankfurt: Suhrkamp, 1973.

Monroe Price and John Wicklein, *Cable Television: A Guide for Citizen Action*, Philadelphia: Pilgrim Press, 1972.

Radical Software (1970-1975).

Michael Shamberg, *Guerrilla Television*, New York: Holt, Rinehart and Winston, 1971.

Andrew Shapiro, *Media Access*, Boston: Little, Brown and Company, 1976.

A.C. Lynn Zelmer, *Community Media Handbook*, Metuchen, NJ: The Scarecrow Press, 1979.

NICARAGUAN VIDEO: 'Live from the Revolution'

Dee Dee Halleck

Any public event in Nicaragua that attracts more than thirty persons will also draw a video crew. Not the US network crews who limit their coverage to interviews with irate *La Prensa* editors and impatient consumers in food lines. Not the European crews who work the solidarity brigades from both East and West Germany. Not the independent US and Canadian crews who line up *en masse* for a Mary Hartman (the nun, not the soap opera dip) tour of La Granja, the model prison farm, or wait for a visit with Ernesto Cardenal at the former Somoza estate, headquarters of the Ministry of Culture. No. The *public* events – the concerts, the neighborhood meetings, the election rallies, the funerals of martyrs, the marches of mothers, the openings of hospitals, the bombing of hospitals, the openings of schools and likewise their attacks by contras, the school graduations, the theatre festivals, the ceremonies for land title distribution to *campesinos*, the Cara Al Pueblo meetings (Face the People) – all these are documented by the video crews of the new Nicaragua. Their work constitutes what is the only authentic video revolution, that much-touted new phenomenon in the world today. Video is part and parcel of the reconstruction of Nicaragua.

Portable video has been an essential tool in recent social struggles in the US, but because the movements it has been a part of are so marginal, it has remained marginally seen – at organizing meetings here and there, on public access cable and late nights on public television. In Nicaragua it is a part of a social dynamic that is transforming a country. Video is not just documenting that process. It is very much a part of that process.

The following are notes from two visits to Nicaragua – in November 1983 and in August 1984. It is also based on information supplied by my son, Ezra, who lives and works in Managua as a video liaison person for X-Change TV, an organization devoted to cultural exchanges between Central America and the US.

The first thing one realizes about Nicaraguan media, and the revolution of which it is a part, is that there is no single party line imposed. This is a diverse society, a nation brought together under a broad coalition of groups, with a wide variety of beliefs and styles. This variety is reflected in the various groups producing and distributing video. There is a different feeling in their work spaces and in the tapes they make.

There are five main centers of production in Nicaragua. The largest and best-equipped is the Sistema Sandinista – the national television system. The second is the video workshop that is part of the Agrarian Reform Ministry – Communicaciones Midinra. The third is Taller Popular De Video (People's Video Workshop), which is a part of the Sandinista Workers Union. The fourth is Incine, under the Ministry of Culture, whose main product is film, but whose work includes video production. The last is Pro-TV, which documents the Cara Al Pueblo meetings and produces programs for the Ministry of Education.

Sistema Sandinista

The Sistema programs two channels every day – one from noon onwards, and the other from 4 pm. The programming, like much of Nicaragua, is an amazing assortment of contradictions – from the saccharine *novelas* from Mexico and Colombia, to the dubbed adventures of Barnaby Jones. It has ads for MacDonalds (yes, there is one in Managua), Coca-Cola and Soviet tractors. In November 1983 the station logo was a group of tiny animated peace doves who flapped their way around a globe to form the letters SSTV as a voice-over, while an accompanying vertical crawl proclaimed 'Toda Las Armas al Pueblo!' (All Arms to the People!). Despite its revolutionary station breaks, the Sistema's productions are often reworking of US network formats. Television everywhere has been so completely dominated by the US model that 'professionalism' has come to be defined as how closely Nicaraguan TV resembles NBC.

The Soviet film that developed in the 1920s was forging new paths and was able to leap over what few conventions existed in film at the time. Nicaraguan TV comes forty years into a TV world in which 180 national TV systems look as though they were all housed on the 40th floor of Rockefeller Center.

The most unusual item on an evening's schedule is apt to be the news, partly because what is happening in Nicaragua is

unusual and interesting, but also because the form in which it is broadcast is apt to be more open-ended and spontaneous than most of the Sistema offerings. Activities are shot hand-held. This doesn't mean they are wiggly. Most of the cameramen (in Nicaragua the Sistema camera people that I saw *were* men) are rock-steady and have no real need for tripods. Their stories are often visual essays – not many interviews and no 'on-the-scene-reporters'. Information is supplied by the newscasters in voice-over, but often long pieces of visual material run without comment – in a style that is leisurely and flowing – more like US public access, where time is free and information isn't sandwiched between commercials. I have the feeling that this is more from lack of enough tightly edited material than from any theoretical concerns of the management. On one news show I saw fifteen minutes of inchoate drunken reveling at the Santo Domingo Festival. Church festivals are always covered. This is a country where the institutional church is in direct opposition to the policies of the government, but where three priests hold cabinet-level positions. All church activities are news: from the Purissima Festival to the bitter pronouncements of anti-Sandinista Arch-bishop Obando Bravo. Participants in the ongoing church debate are endlessly interviewed in the TV studios. On most nights the church is at least a third of the news.

The segments on the news that are produced in the studio are often awkward and replete with transitional errors and shaky chroma-key edges. The occasional goofs and missed cues have made the administration of the Sistema reluctant to distribute their news programs abroad. X-Change TV has repeatedly tried to get samples of the news for distribution, but Sistema executives would rather lend out their 'professional' work – slick entertainment specials – in the 'Live-from-Lincoln-Center' genre. These canned and controlled artsy shows are a long way from the 'live-from-the-revolution' programs that X-Change has in mind. But the Sistema is probably ashamed of the news. The open informality may charm Northern visitors, the transitional goofs may denote self-referential process consciousness to a *Screen* subscriber, but they only give ulcers to the Sistema's producers.

The attraction of X-Change to the more primitive news is an example of the kind of solidarity activity that has been one element of an ongoing debate within the Ministry of Culture and the artistic community in Managua. One of the results of the revolution has been an explosion of creativity among the campesinos; naive writing and primitive painting have proliferated. This type of art is always popular with solidarity groups. A German art gallery sponsored huge editions of primitive painting posters – reproduced on expensive paper with an elaborate graphic technique. Likewise, editions of campesino poetry, produced by internationalists, have been printed and bound and distributed widely. The national folklorico dance movement is doing great, receiving donations from all over the world. But professional artists have asked: where, in this scheme, is the support for serious artists who may be developing a more complex and probing aesthetic? The attraction of revolutionary tourists for primitive posters leaves out Nicaraguan artists who have spent long careers in the arts. In a country where every piece of paper and every pencil is a precious resource, the Ministry of Culture cannot afford to put out editions of *their* works. Economic concerns are not the only issue, as there are many who believe that the arts should be mass-based and that supporting an elite group of university-trained artists only perpetuates the class differences that still exist from pre-revolutionary times.

While the debate continues, an important role of the Sistema has been to make national performance of both the folklorico and the professional theatre and dance groups available to a wide audience. *Sandino-Santo Y Seña* (Saint and Symbol), their most elaborate presentation to date, is a dance and music spectacular that was recorded at a live performance in a ruined hotel that has recently become the opera house of Managua. The building is a crumbling shell with an eery presence that forms a poignant reminder that this is NOT a typical theatre in a typical Latin American country, but constitutes an art built on the destruction of resistant traditions. I saw a performance there in August, where the vigor and enthusiasm of the production burst through the decay of the surroundings. The technical virtuosity of the lighting, the dancing and the hundred-piece string(!) orchestra was in stark contrast to the extreme poverty of most of the audience and with the decrepit state of the theatre. Imagine that an earthquake has

photo: DeeDee Halleck

A state-owned theatre, previously owned by the Somoza family

destroyed the Plaza Hotel and you are sitting in its ruins watching Ballet Hispanico with an audience of three thousand unemployed workers from the South Bronx. Needless to say, there are a few differences. For one thing, because of the revolution, the theatre is THEIR theatre. You feel it when you are there with them. That sense of empowerment is a part of the event; it is also a part of the TV presentations that record it. The audience cutaways are therefore different. They serve the function of reminding the TV audience of just whose show it is anyway. (Come to think of it, maybe the Lincoln Center cutaways serve the same purpose . . .)

Midinra

Communicaciones Midinra is part of the Agrarian Ministry. The offices are a little outside of Managua on the road to Masaya, in what was a rather well-to-do hacienda-type house with a large interior patio surrounded by grandiose archways. When I was last there the patio was being used to store empty VCR boxes. Below the arches, the desks and files are an amazing collection of types – from Danish Modern to Ramada Inn Inquisition style. Their walnut and teak finishes are stencilled in prominent places like subway graffiti tags with huge numbers in bright red and white paint. The numbers designate which farm the furniture was confiscated from. Many of the large farms in Nicaragua were abandoned after the revolution and the confiscated property from these *ranchos* gives Midinra a material edge among the video groups. Desks and files they may have, but the office desperately needs more telephones. Over seventy persons work there, and their single telephone is the kind of frustrating bottleneck through which any work in present-day Nicaragua must eventually pass.

Video isn't the only thing that Midinra does. They have several printing presses and do the work of documenting and explaining the agrarian reform process. Their primary aim is making the agrarian reform work understood by and available to the peasants and farm workers in the countryside, and secondarily informing a wider public – city dwellers in Managua, Leon and Granada, but also other countries and international organizations. Several of their publications are in English. Arturo Zamora is director of Communicaciones Midinra. It is indicative of his self-effacing style that he has no desk or office, but hangs out from work space to work space jumping up apologetically to give this or that worker back his or her seat. Arturo directs the printing, audio-visual and video. The audio-visual is a large department with a still-photo darkroom for both color and black and white. They have produced over a dozen slide shows with synchronized tracks. Subjects include 'The Benefits of Soy Beans' and 'Nutrition for Pregnant Women'. Midinra is planning an audio studio and hopes to do a regular radio series in the near future.

The video department consists of four rooms – an editing room, a tape library, an equipment room and an office. Needless to say, the office is the furthest from the air-conditioner. In Nicaragua, equipment and tapes are treated with the utmost respect. This is not mystified Third World awe, but a concrete understanding of the hassles involved in part-replacement and tape purchase. Augusto Tablada is director of the video department. He likes to tell how he was caught in monsoon-type rains in an open field with their new Sony N-3 camera and a 4800 VCR deck. He took off his rain gear and put it as additional protection over the already plastic-encased equipment, and spent seven hours in pouring rain trying to hold the equipment out of the mud. 'The camera costs dollars,' he grins. 'I'm only worth cordobas.' Exchange dollars are practically impossible to get, and cordobas won't buy equipment. All of the video groups in Nicaragua rely heavily on donated equipment.

Midinra films are available in both 3/4 and Beta. Most production is shot and edited on 3/4, then transferred to Beta for distribution to the countryside. Each regional headquarters has a Beta player and has regular showings of Midinra tapes. They also show work by US independents and even a few Hollywood films. *Julia* was going to the mountains on the week I was there.

Miriam Carrero comes to work at Midinra with a shopping bag full of powdered milk. The boxes have a smiling blond and blue-eyed toddler on the front. The lettering on the box is Cyrillic: the milk is Russian. Powdered milk from the US is difficult to get here. All US products are harder and harder to get. Miriam has two children – a four-month-old baby and a three-year-old girl. Her mother assists in the childcare, as in many Nicaraguan extended families, but even so, working as a video editor is difficult with two young ones. Miriam gets up at 5 am to go to the market to be sure she can get the week's supply of powdered milk for the baby. Miriam started out in film work at Incine. She recently changed, initially because the pay was better; Incine pays only 3,700 cordobas a month ($130) while Midinra gives 6,000. Now Miriam is very enthusiastic about video and wants to learn all aspects of production. She now runs the editing machines but is very much involved in content decisions. From what I could gather of the post-production process, tapes at Midinra evolve organically (to use an agricultural term) from the material collected. The camera person works with the editor. Input can come from many persons at Midinra and the atmosphere is that of a collective, not a hierarchy. Technical advice is supplied on occasion by agricultural advisors; for example, a cattle geneticist was working closely on a recent tape on cattle production.

Midinra's work is primarily focused on agrarian topics, but, like Jaime Wheelock, director of the Agrarian ministry, their interests extend to theoretical and historical issues as well. Midinra recently completed an historical tape to commemorate the 50-year anniversary of Sandino's death. This tape is a mixture of archive footage, recent war footage and agrarian images. Of all the tapes I have seen from Nicaragua, it takes the most risks. It is a passionate experimental tape, using Eisenstein-type montage juxtapositions to rev up emotions. (After a shot of a US helicopter being shot down, there is a close-up of a bull being castrated.) This anniversary was the focus of a series on the Sistema. Each of the *comandantes* had hour-long interviews in which they answered questions posed to them by the Sistema. Midinra took Jaime Wheelock to the countryside, where he discussed the issues with the *campesinos*. They then edited this into an hour program and wanted the Sistema to run that instead of the stuffy studio format interview. The television system refused to air it, saying it did not fit their series. (This type of evasion is a familiar story to independents who try to deal with US public TV.) Actually the relationship of Midinra to the Sistema is one of the more baffling issues for an outsider to comprehend. Midinra has to BUY time on the Sistema: 60,000 cordobas for each hour of program. They do a monthly program, but all the time is paid for, and their programs are subject (as in the interview case) to rejection by the management.

Midinra has been a haven for foreign independents. Its open atmosphere and friendly workers have made it a place where US independent filmmakers could align their cameras, splice light cables or just hang out and screen tapes. In a sense, Midinra's video grew out of the independent movement in the US. Prior to 1979, Augusto spent time in the US and worked with Eddie Becker, an independent producer in Washington. After the revolution, Eddie came to Midinra to help train agricultural workers in video skills. The students from his class are still the mainstays of video people at Midinra. Eddie found that they picked up camera techniques quite easily. What he ended up spending most of his time teaching was how to make a good solder. He brought with him three connector kit bags from Radio Shack and several hundred yards of cable. The cables they produced are still in use. A trouble-shooting manual that he designed for them is the basic handbook of their equipment room.

Most internationalist media people sooner or later find their way out of the Carretera Masaya to Midinra's workshop. Before they leave, they are given a list of missing parts and needed equipment to send back. Video people from Germany have been active in their support of Midinra and have raised money from trade unions for essential equipment. A major effort is underway at the present time to do a TV series with West Germany; Miriam is co-producing it with a woman producer from Munich. This show will be a docu-drama series on farm life. It is a children's series: the

photo: Eddie Becker

Augusto Tablada, Director of Video for Communicaciones Midinra, on location in 1981.

Miriam Loasita edits a tape on milk production at Communicaciones Midinra.

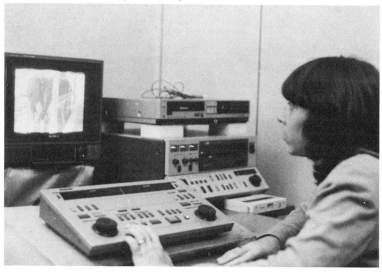

photo: Dee Dee Halleck

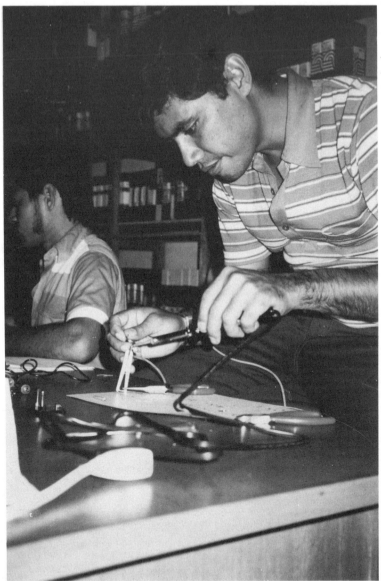

photo: Eddie Becker

A member of Eddie Becker's soldering workshop at Communicaciones Midinra.

first program shows a young boy visiting his grandfather on a coffee farm. The grandfather explains in detail just how things have changed since the revolution.

Midinra would like to develop their co-production possibilities. They have been aghast at the enormous sums of money that US (and Canadian and European) producers spend on equipping a production in Nicaragua. Arturo suggests, 'Why not use our equipment and work in co-production with us? That way we can all benefit.' Arturo recently assisted Bianca Jagger on a documentary about ecology in Nicaragua for distribution in the US. Just as with their printed materials, Midinra sees their audience as including not only Nicaraguans. 'We want to do our part to counter the dis-information that the world hears about Nicaragua,' Arturo explains. He has embarked on a series called *Alternative Views* (not to be confused with the Austin cable show of the same name) to begin to counter Western press bias. This type of production could also be done as co-productions, he feels.

Future plans at Midinra include a feature film on the history of Sandino. Wilfredo Ortega Mercado, who is currently the tape librarian, has a plan for a program on cultural seduction – how young campesinos lose their minds to American consumer goods. Miriam hopes to produce a program on women agricultural workers. And the ongoing work continues – the documentation of land reform, the construction of cooperative dairies, the research into ecological methods of pest control and health care in rural areas. Midinra also serves as a liaison from the producer to the consumer. Of their tapes that have been most popular here in the US as part of the X-Change TV series, two are on very parochial specific topics: *Qué Pasa Con El Papel Higiénico*, and *Qué Pasa Con Las Papas*. The first, 'What's Up with the Toilet Paper?', is a sort of point-counterpoint about why there isn't enough toilet paper in the country. Why the shortage? Humorous and catchy interviews with people on the street convey the range of feeling about toilet paper. There IS a real shortage in Nicaragua, and this lack has become one of the major complaints by the sectors of the population that are most against the revolution. By repeating these complaints and disseminating them, Midinra itself has been criticized. The criticism against the tape only increased its popularity, and the tape became an important element in the ongoing discussions about shortages, hoarding and rationing. The second tape is about potatoes. Potatoes grow well in Nicaragua, but poor farming methods have slowed production. This is a tape in praise of the potato that includes instructions for successful harvests.

Taller Popular

Taller Popular de Video Timoteo Velasquez is a workshop named for a fallen comrade. It is part of the Central Sandinista de Trabajadores (CST), the largest union in Nicaragua. Like Midinra, they also have a regular series on the Sistema, and also distribute via Betamax to union locals throughout the country. It is housed and shares resources with Tercer Cine, a private production company composed of Jackie Reiter, Wolf Tirado and Jan Kees de Rooy. The Taller began as a Super 8 workshop taught by Julia LeSage. She went to Nicaragua in 1981 on a special project sponsored by the United Nations. 'We worked mostly on editing techniques and alternatives to synch sound interviews, such as the use of music, other taped verbal material and background sound. At the suggestion of Amina Luna, one of the CST filmmakers, we began filming a project on working women's participation in the revolution, which the group has since completed in video.'

Super 8 processing soon became too difficult, as Kodak withdrew all trade with Nicaragua. The workshop now works almost entirely in video. Amina is still one of the producers, along with Francisco Sanchez, Oscar Ortiz and Ileana Estreber. Their productions center on people – close shots of faces alternating with their homes, their land, their work. *Así Avanzamos* is a tape about a cattle collective, faced with all the problems of building up production, together with the stresses and material losses of the contra-inflicted war damage. The determination of the people to keep on working ('Asi Avanzamos' – so we advance) is evident on their hopeful faces. There is a dreamy, romantic quality to many of the Taller productions. This is not, however, the romantic view of 'primitive' life that we sometimes find in the work of Gringo anthropologist/filmmakers. The faces of the people emanate a hope that is reinforced by the real accomplishments they have gained in the face of incredible odds. The ease with which the peasants *participate* with the video production gives the discourse an intimacy that transcends the interview format. This *sharing* with the videomakers is what characterizes the work of US independent Skip Blumberg. There is a one-to-one relationship with the camera that is as close as video can get to an authentic human relationship. This intimacy can, on occasion, make the Taller tapes deeply tragic. *Las Mujeres* is about two women who work in the reconstruction in one of the northern areas. They describe some of the hardships they have encountered in their work, but go on to list the accomplishments of the literacy campaign and the agrarian reform work in the face of the fear and intimidation that the contras impose. The bravery of these two women included their willingness to talk with the video crew. Shortly after the tape appeared on television, they were both killed – brutally murdered. One was tortured and raped along with her six children. This type of contra terror is not unusual; their targets are those who work with the revolution. The contras rarely attack the army. Instead they go after the schoolteachers, the doctors, the nurses and agrarian reform workers – and, on occasion, those peasants who share their hope and dedication with a video crew.

Incine

Incine is the film production unit of the Ministry of Culture. It was born under fire in the mountains before the revolution. I talked with Noel Rivera, who was one of the 'muchachos' who formed the mainstay of the army of insurrection. He was only 15 years old when he left home to fight against Somoza's National Guard. In his battalion was a film crew, which needed someone to run the Nagra, the basic audio recorder used for film documentaries. He became the sound man after a few days training and has worked with Incine ever since. Incine has made one feature –*Alcinor and the Condor* – a co-production with Costa Rica, Mexico and Cuba, and many documentaries. Their newsreels are often shown before the feature films in the theatres around the country. Half of the theatres in Managua are privately owned and Incine has to pay for the time for newsreel projection. The theatre owners refuse to play shorts that are longer than ten minutes. Noel recounts the story of a newsreel he helped make that was twelve minutes long. When he saw it at the theatre, it was strangely truncated. The theatre owner had just lopped off the last two minutes of the documentary in mid-sentence.

Movie theatres in Managua show the same junk films that we get on Times Square. Kung Fu movies are the most popular and audiences line up at 7:30 am to see a 9:30 show on Saturday morning. The Cinemateca is a state-owned theatre that shows a few Eastern European films (Czech, Hungarian) and occasionally an independent feature from the US. Cuban films draw large crowds.

Incine has a video department directed by Rosanne Lacayo. The Lacayos are the main force behind Incine and some have accused the organization of being a family affair. Their most recent tape is a homage to Julio Cortezar, poet and friend to the Nicaraguan revolution. Within the cultural debate mentioned earlier, Incine stands squarely with the 'serious art' contingent.

Their main interest lies in producing film versions of Latin American novels.

Incine has been on the receiving end of lavish gifts of production equipment and production assistance. The immediate successes of ICAIC, the Cuban film production institute, led many to hope that Nicaragua's film production would accomplish similar feats. Several factors mitigate against this. The most important is the strain and pressures of the war situation in Nicaragua. Except for the Bay of Pigs fiasco and the imposed economic constraints, Cuba has not had to withstand the brutal forces of reaction that attack Nicaragua daily. Second, and certainly a part of the first, is the worsening economic situation, with the price of film and processing in Mexican Laboratories rising daily. Third is more internal to Incine. Their organization seems the most chaotic of the media groups that I visited. Incine is built on grandiose schemes that get hung up in the simplest of details. While I was there, a group of technicians from Los Angeles were sponsoring technical workshops. The group came with a large donation of lights and equipment. They were surprised at the lack of the most *basic* tools, however, and were unable to use most of their lights. There was only one circuit capable of running ONE of their lights in the workshop building. These workshops were funded by the Common Sense Foundation. Perhaps they could have had more common sense and have been more utilitarian in scope. But quien sabe? Maybe some nascent cinematographer was tapped by the classes and will emerge as a leader of the budding Nicaraguan film industry. In the meantime, the video production unit is becoming more and more important as a center of activity at Incine.

Cara al Pueblo

The other video production unit is the audio-visual department of the Department of the Interior. A unit from this department produces weekly Cara Al Pueblo meetings and also does production for the Ministry of Education – both documentation and tapes for instructional purposes. The Cara Al Pueblo are weekly meetings of the *comandantes* with the people – in the barrios around Managua and in the countryside. These are perhaps the most characteristic public events of the revolution; they are to Nicaragua what Fidel's speeches are to Cuba. It is a significant difference that these are two-way – not the voice of a single leader, but the questions of the people directed to a group of their leaders. These may include local leaders, the directors of the local block associations. The questions range from specifics on the new sewer lines for the neighborhood to more philosophical questions on the relationship between church and state. When the meetings are held in Managua, they are broadcast live from a mobile van. These programs are very popular and would have high ratings if the Sistema bothered to measure that. There have been accusations that these meetings are orchestrated by the local CDSs (neighborhood committees for defense of the revolution), and that only acceptable questions are allowed, but the shows I saw were spontaneous and often highly critical of the government. The Cara Al Pueblo meetings will become increasingly important as economic conditions worsen. Their value is not as a safety valve, but as an effective way for people to have input into national decisions. The degree to which these meetings express the authentic fears, angers and hopes of the people will be an important measure of public accountability. This process is very much the national dialogue, and the participation of video is crucial. The Cara Al Pueblo has a well-equipped van which is the envy of the other video producers of Managua. One of the ironies of the situation there is that, despite the collaborative attitude at the highest level of government, there exists among departments a great deal of competition and possessiveness. These is very little communication among the various organizations. Incine has no idea of what Midinra is doing. Midinra has no way to gauge their schedule on the Sistema, because they are not privy to the Sistema's long-range planning and do not know month-to-month where their slot will be positioned. The Taller has no contact with Incine. They have only one 4800 portable recording deck. If that is in the repair shop, they have to cancel all their shoots – even though there are at least six other decks that could be loaned from other workshops. There is only one engineer who works at the Sistema who has put his job on the line by sometimes sneaking a workshop deck into his shop to repair. There are healthy aspects to the independence of the various groups – there is no monolithic look to Nicaraguan video – but all the groups would benefit more from more sharing of resources.

It is sobering to contemplate the future of Nicaraguan video. Even if the vicious Contra War stops (which would happen almost immediately if the US stopped funding it), the economic situation is so difficult that conditions will probably worsen in the short run. As the dollar pinch gets harder, there will be increased struggles within the trade unions. Rampant inflation has hit most workers, even though the prices of staples are fixed. Midinra, Incine, the Sistema and the Cara al Pueblo are all part of the government.

They are the 'voice of the people' only in so far as the government remains true to the ideals and aspirations of the revolution. As a voice of the workers, Taller Popular de Video may play an increasingly important role in articulating their needs and dissatisfactions. The real work of the revolution is in the future and video can play a constructive role in so far as expression retains authenticity and pluralism.

The US independent community has been an important source for Nicaraguan video – a source for technical assistance, for equipment donations and for programming exchange. But perhaps most important has been the inspiration of video use. The kind of personal human community video that has characterized our marginalized independent video work here in the US has become the standard for a video community in Nicaragua whose cameras are the eyes of their nation, and whose nation stands at the heart of current human history.

Note

A version of this article first appeared in the November 1984 issue of *The Independent* in the USA.

THE REUTERS FACTOR
Myths and Realities of Communicology: A Scenario

Michael Chanan

I

The year is 1848. A young German Jewish intellectual involved in radical journalism is obliged to leave his homeland, and heads for Paris. He is the third son of the Provisional Rabbi of Cassel. At the beginning of the decade he had settled in Berlin, where he was baptised and married the daughter of a banker. Assisted by his father-in-law's capital, he bought a share in an established bookshop and publishing business which then, under his guidance, brought out a number of 'democratic' pamphlets in the year of the Revolution.

In Paris, he joins the staff of a news agency owned by another Jew of letters, Charles Havas; he works as a translator. A year later he leaves his employer and sets up his own rival news-sheet. It fails, and he moves to Aachen, where, on 1st October 1849, Europe's first commercial telegraph line opens: the Prussian State Telegraph line from Berlin. He sets up in business supplying local clients with the news from the Prussian capital, soon expanding to supply clients in Antwerp and Brussels. When the French open a line the following spring from Brussels to Paris, he bridges the gap – first with carrier pigeons, and then with horses. But competition is fierce. In Berlin, another Jewish ex-Havas employee, Bernhard Wolff by name, has set up an agency with the backing of the electrical entrepreneur Werner Siemens. One day Siemens meets our hero, and advises him to go and start a cable agency in London. Born Samuel Levi Josaphat, he is known to history by his baptised name, Paul Julius Reuter.

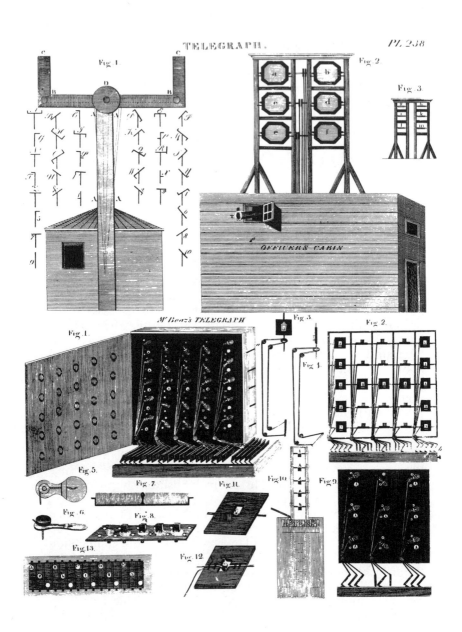

II

One of the myths that has built up around high technology is the vision of a completely wired-up society. Everyone's home is to be wired in through their television sets and computers to other computers, which are wired in, in turn, to still more computers, and everyone and everything is fully programmed. You've not just got all the home entertainment you could want, you're also in instant two-way communication with the whole world. You've no need to go out shopping because you can order things and even pay for them through your tv set, and then consult your bank manager at the touch of a button. You'll even – they tell you – be able to work from home. You'll never need to step outside your front door, but if you want to, you'll have portable extensions to all your devices, so you need never be without their wonderful convenience.

This is the vision which is promoted by the government of Mrs Thatcher – according to what Home Secretary Leon Brittan said in a BBC Television 'Panorama' report on cable tv (20th February 1984). These people see everything linked in together in a comprehensive system, designed to distribute pre-packaged dollops of entertainment and 'information' on a strictly commercial commodity basis: a 'free market' which they know perfectly well is loaded in favour of authority. They believe this wired-up society is inevitable because the technology for it is already there – a self-fulfilling prophecy as old as capitalism – and they look to the business of developing it as to a panacea. The vulgar materialists among them simply see it as the thing to get into – the fastest growing sector of production with the biggest surplus profits. But in the eyes of the idealists, whether romantics or philosophers, it will renovate the infrastructure, the forms and institutions, the mode of operation, which govern the way things are done, even the way people think, because it will give people new ways to process and communicate information; and it will thus assist their project, which is to restructure the British economy, and reverse the decline of British capitalism.

The new infrastructure will be formed by both extending and replacing different parts of the old, fragmenting and parcelling out bits of state-owned enterprise according to the scheme of the day. They have separated British Telecom, for example, from the Post Office, to make ready for the process they call privatisation. Now, as I write, tv commercials are advertising the prospectus for the sale of British Telecom. There's even been talk of selling off the BBC.

They must know (but never let on if they do) that there will be masses of people excluded from participation in this heaven on earth. They are therefore equally set on devising ways of keeping these masses under control, and of nipping rebellion in the bud. Those who warn about the technology of social control which is now being introduced into the police force are right to do so. The police state and the information society are constructed on the same foundations and by the same means. This much is probably already apparent to anyone who reads the newspapers and watches television, for all their disinformation. But the issues this process raises are a minefield, and many disturbing notions seep through the public discourse. One paradox is that a welter of articles and programmes proclaim the new technology as a means of what the hacks have the nerve to call 'liberation' and 'democratisation' – both an end to the drudgery of work and a new promise of instant participation; and yet in Britain in 1984, the real accompaniment to all the talk of an astonishing future is the famous return to Victorian morality of the Thatcherites. Very well, then, let's go back to the nineteenth century, and look at where the new technology started.

III

The apologists are right about one thing. The age of entrepreneurial capitalism didn't just consist of fortunes made from new industrial processes; it also saw the birth of modern communications. Communications are an integral part of the capitalist mode of production. First there's the development of the physical conditions: as goods came to be distributed in distant markets and foreign raw materials were increasingly employed in production, especially those that could be cheaply extracted from the expanding colonies, the improvement of terrestrial transport, which in feudal society was unorganised, became imperative. In due course, 'the feverish haste of production, its enormous extent, its constant flinging of capital and labour from one sphere of production into another, and its newly-created connections with the markets of the whole world' (Marx, p. 384), also make improved communications imperative for another reason: it creates a generalised need for the dissemination of a new type of information, consisting in stock market quotations, raw materials prices, credit rates, statistics and news.

In short, by the early 19th century the growth of capitalism had created pressing needs for improved commercial intelligence. The two went hand in hand. Between 1800 and 1913, as modern communications were developing, the value of world trade expanded (according to one estimate) more than twenty-five fold, from £320m to £8360m. The relationship between the two is an aspect of what we can call the Reuters Factor, which functions like a multiplier that turns an increase in the supply of information into an increase in business.

Big banking houses like Rothschild's started off with their own communications systems, using couriers and carrier pigeons. Newspapers like *The Times* set up networks to provide regular

Reuter's first news venture, in 1850, included a pigeon post between Aachen and Brussels. In 1944, Reuters' pigeons brought news from the Normandy beachhead.

information on market prices in different financial centres, and Havas in France made the reputation upon which he built his news agency by supplying the Bourse with the European exchange rates. On the day that the Prussians opened a state telegraph line between Berlin and Aachen, 1st October 1849, two new contenders, both of whom started with Havas, set up in business: Bernhard Wolff in Berlin and, at the other end, with an overland link to Paris, Paul Julius Reuter. As the telegraph network was extended, Reuter preceded it, and in 1851, he established himself in London in order to exploit the submarine link between Calais and Dover.

The process which is described in the present essay is coextensive with the trajectory which Reuters has followed since, from its inception to the present day, when it's become a success story in the application of the latest communications technologies. Although, as we saw, it begins as a conventional business undertaking, Reuters' trajectory has been far from conventionally typical of capitalist growth (what is, when you come down to it?). But its very singularities make it typical in a kind of unconventional way: its discovery that news is a very peculiar kind of commodity, the question of its relationship to the authority of the State, its changing structure of ownership, from entrepreneurial to corporate. All these things, upon examination, draw our attention to internal features of capitalism which are frequently invisible. We find we're dealing with the bloodstream of the system: the flow of information upon which the health of the body depends. News is only part of this.

Reuter realized very early that the supply of news to newspapers by itself could not succeed in generating a profit. For one thing, the newspapers were jealous of their own prerogatives, especially, in London, *The Times*. But the Stock Exchange was a different matter, and Reuters' first English clients were private commercial subscribers. From biographical information (Storey), it is clear that Reuter understood something of the ideological relation between news and commercial information; he knew, for example, that he couldn't compete with the newspaper correspondents' form of comment, interpretation and graphic description. Telegraphy was too expensive. So he emphasised the telegraph's advantages of speed and conciseness, and constructed a model of reporting 'facts' which came from the criteria of commercial usage, where it was pretty unambiguous – the facts had numbers attached to them. He also talked about objectivity – which was pure expediency. He was a foreigner reporting imperialist wars and diplomacy, so he couldn't afford to incur the displeasure of

Her Majesty's Government. He was also trying to satisfy the varying political and ideological inclinations of different newspapers.

To serve the interests of Empire and of them all, Reuter devised a code of practices for his establishment which succeeded in meeting all prejudices. It has essentially changed very little since it emerged in the 1860s and 70s, and lies at the basis of modern bourgeois ideologies of journalism. This is hardly accidental. Reuters made itself essential to the growing press, especially the growing number of provincial newspapers, unable to afford their own foreign news reporting services, who came together in the Press Association in 1865. The relationship was sealed in an agreement by which the Press Association provided the information for Reuters' cables to overseas clients. (The partnership strengthened Reuters internationally too, and this was the period when the big international agencies were carving up the world among them.) Subsequently, the Press Association were to join the Fleet Street newspaper proprietors in corporate ownership of Reuters, to preserve its independence.

For all this, news for the press alone was no way to make the venture a success. Periodically, throughout its history, Reuters has made investments in the improvement of its basic activities in commercial intelligence. They include especially the acquisition in 1943 of Comtelburo, a commercial and financial service designed to meet the needs mainly of banks and commercial institutions. The introduction over the last decade of specialist computerised financial services, transmitted worldwide by satellite, has turned Reuters into a nest-egg for the company's owners. Masters of an industry in deep trouble – partly brought on by the havoc which new technologies wreak upon its traditional labour processes – they decided to do some selling off when they realized that Reuters was now one of Britain's largest companies, with a valuation of £1 billion. They've of course been doing their damnedest to keep the whole thing low profile.

IV

In Britain, communications, by ancient and semi-inviolable conventions, were a monopoly of the crown. Her Majesty's mails were transported and delivered by Her Majesty's servants. The revenue from the post was income for Her Majesty's Government. The expansion of newspapers in the course of the 18th century had depended on the growth of more effective communications; the development of the press was intimately linked with the improve-

Julius de Reuter Statue outside Royal Exchange.

ment of roads, and especially the growing efficiency of the General Post Office, through which newspapers were distributed. The need to rectify abuses of the system had at times contributed to the improvements.

But communications have also always been a matter for the military. Claude Chappe's semaphore telegraph, first introduced by order of Robespierre and the Committee of Public Safety in 1793, gave Napoleon the best military intelligence system in Europe. By the beginning of the 19th century (when the electric battery was invented), semaphore telegraph stations stretched out across the hills, passing messages at considerable speeds: just over four minutes from Calais to Paris, and less than a quarter of an hour from Toulon. They consisted of tall posts holding a pair of thin semaphore arms silhouetted against the sky so that the operator at the next station several miles away could read the signals clearly through his telescope. Torches on the arms made it possible to send messages by night. But the system was cumbersome. The distance between stations was limited by the range of the telescopes. It also required foolproof drill and a signal manual. For such a system to be commercially practical, one of the things it lacked was a simple, easy and efficient form of transmission code, which could be operated by ordinary paid employees. By about 1860 this great semaphore system had been replaced by the electric telegraph.

The telegraph was the first commercially successful application of the new science of electro-magnetism. Electricity came into commercial and industrial use during the course of the 19th century for communication, light and power, in that order. But the successful application of the telegraph involved two aspects: first there was the physical business of sending and receiving signals electro-magnetically. This achievement was the fruit of scores of workers, many of them scientists of lasting fame (Wheatstone, Gauss, Weber, Henry), investigating between them a series of interconnected problems such as current generation, propagation of the current through wires, electrical measurement and so forth. Secondly, there was the ingenuity needed to find the most effective code for transmitting messages in the technically appropriate form of discrete signals, a problem of mathematical logic. A solution, almost universally adopted within a short number of years, was provided in 1832 by an amateur – something that was still possible in those days. A portrait painter by profession, Samuel Morse translated the alphabet into a series of variously combined short or long pulses which gave the dots and dashes of an easily mastered digital code, in a manner so elegant that it still survives.

It is enough to put it this way – to refer to certain technical properties of the system – to anticipate a succession of problems of this kind which the development of communications technologies repeatedly throw up, whose study is nowadays, among other things, the domain of information theory. This is the academic discipline, mathematically based, concerned with the logical properties of transmitted messages: questions of redundancy, noise, interference, the difference between the digital and the analogue and so forth. This theoretical framework, however, is only very recent – which reminds us that throughout the history of capitalism such problems have usually been solved in practice before they were even posed in theory. The invention and application of the first generation of modern communications was achieved without it.

The intellectual basis of modern information theory lies in the quite unconnected work at the end of this period of mathematicians and logicians like Boole, or Russell and Whitehead, whose work is also the basis of the computer sciences. Of course the idea of the computer is much older. Blaise Pascal, mathematician and mystic, built the first mechanical calculating machine in the mid-17th century.

Two hundred years later, at the very moment, as Harold Perkin puts it, as 'the minimal, decentralised, regulatory, laissez-faire State of the entrepreneurial ideal was consolidating itself as the norm of political theory, the expanding, centralised, bureaucratic, interventionist State of modern times was coming into being in its administrative practices' (Perkin, p. 319). The corresponding expansion in statistics and computation imposed severe strains on their established mode of production. The annual Greenwich nautical tables, for example, were produced on an outwork system, by individual human computers. (Until the 20th century, the word 'computer' referred to a human being.) Some were highly skilled, but most computation at the time was done by provincial clergymen, who lived on the Bible and seven-figure logarithms, did all their work by hand, and were only too apt to make mistakes. To remedy the problem of productivity and accuracy, a Cambridge professor of mathematics conceived the idea of doing it all mechanically, on a machine called an analytical engine. Charles Babbage's efforts were at first backed by the government but ended up in a great Victorian folly which never fulfilled its purpose; it now lies in the Science Museum as a relic. But it was, in its conception, as the poet Hans Magnus Enzensberger describes it,

The first digital computer,
with no vacuum tubes, no transistor.
Weighing fifty tonnes,
as big as a room, a gearwork of brass,
pewter, and steel, driven by springs
and weights,
capable of any computation whatsoever,
even of playing chess,
or composing sonatas . . .

(C.B. (1792–1871) in *Mausoleum)*

A third antecedent is the logical idea of a 'universal machine' conceived by a young English mathematician in the 1930s, an immediate conceptual precursor of the electronic computer: the Turing Machine. It needed the Second World War, however, and the impulse of the military quest for a new generation of communications technologies, for computer science and information theory to come into existence. They accompany the development of television, radar, rocketry, nuclear weapons, satellites, telecommunication and microelectronics. And also the hubris of the search by academics and scientists in r&d laboratories, for something called artificial intelligence.

V

The new telegraphic news of the 19th century played an enormous role in shaping the sensibilities of the new and evolving industrial press. The total circulation of daily papers in the UK in 1854 was less than 100,000, of which *The Times* claimed 51,000. Sixteen years later, during the Franco-Prussian War, The *Daily News* alone had 150,000, and the editor of *The Times*, Mowbray Morris, instructed his correspondents abroad that the telegraph had superseded the newsletter and had rendered necessary a different style and treatment of public subjects. These sixteen years cover a tale of resistance by *The Times* to Reuters' growing monopoly in the provision of foreign news to the country's press. But not only was Reuters zealous about its special reputation for accuracy and trustworthiness, *The Times* was finally forced to give in when Reuters also proved more efficient and resourceful in the process of news gathering itself.

One effect of telegraphic reporting, due to the rapidity of transmission, was to establish a daily 24-hour cycle in the production of the news. Indeed, the new simultaneity of events threatened chaos in many departments of the social superstructure, which could only be put in order by international co-operation.

The standardisation of the clock around the world was indexed, by international agreement which records the British imperial supremacy of the epoch, to London and the Royal Observatory in Greenwich. It's a symbolic moment in modern history. You could almost say it represents a definitive break with the past, a change in the very measure of history. From now on, it will be possible not only vastly to improve the regulation of prices, but also to record exactly the moment at which events take place.

A delusion will grow: that it is a real gain in the quality of life to be able to take more effective control of time by measuring it ever more precisely. Such a delusion is fuelled by the growing precision of science. Soon, 'scientific management' will appear – the technique of timing the segments of the worker's labour process by which the output of his or her labour power may be more precisely measured. It is also highly relevant that this new regulation of time – and subsequently, similar international treaties concerned with the regulation of the flow of information in different media – transcends the barriers between nations, from *Realpolitik* to Cold War. The one thing opposing factions do not entirely break off are the channels of communication. The great problem is how to control them, how to prevent the enemy hearing what you don't want him to, how to monitor the enemy's communications, and how to influence his interpretation of what you let him hear. It is significant that the pioneering work in which Alan Turing was engaged during the war, which led to the construction of the first electronic computers at the end of the 40s, was the application of electronics to the mathematical art of code-breaking. (And curious that Turing should have been another eccentric English mathematician.)

VI

Nor did the telegraph serve capitalist interests only passively. By linking distant markets together, the telegraph turned them into one vast interdependent market, in which a change in price in one part affected the whole system at once. As it advanced beyond the frontiers of the traditional markets, the telegraph helped to extend the geographical reach of capitalism. It also helped to intensify its operation. As a result of penny postage, railways, telegraphy, in short, the whole improved means of communication (as Marx observed in *Capital*), Britain already carried out five to six times more business with about the same circulation of bank notes. (It was Charles Babbage, several times cited by Marx in *Capital* as an authority on such matters, who persuaded Rowland Hill to introduce the flat-rate penny post in 1840, when he proved conclusively that the cost of collecting, stamping and delivering a letter was far greater than the cost of transporting it, and Post Office operations would be, as we should now say, streamlined, by a charge independent of the distance carried. Enzensberger refers to Marx 'checking the arithmetic and finding it correct'.) In short, new and improved means of communication were not just a range of products which entrepreneurial capitalism produced in its factories, but a necessary part of its social means of production. More accurately, they constituted an infrastructure, which stands to the individual producer as a precondition to his own undertaking, though at the same time this infrastructure is a product of the whole ensemble of individual enterprises.

Being an infrastructure, however, the development of communications constitute a problem for the development of the capitalist mode of production. They consist in *general conditions of production* which, as Marx explained in the *Grundrisse*, presuppose a stage of development of the forces of production and private capital for which their improvement is itself a necessary condition. Because of this, the matter becomes a special object of interest on the part of the state, in its role of overseer and arbiter of social development in the interests of the capitalist class; and thus it undertakes the necessary enterprises which at any given moment the capitalist class left to itself is unable to. This is already to be seen in Prussian and French government sponsorship of the first telegraph lines. It is a role, however, to which the state has to learn to adapt. When one of the inventors of telegraphy, a man by the name of Ronalds, quite naturally, in 1816, offered his services to the Admiralty, they declined. Half a century later, with anarchic competition between the different private telegraph networks leading to economic chaos, the British government decided to act, and empowered the Post Office to take over the entire telegraph system. It was the first nationalisation.

VII

In 1944, the North American business magazine *Fortune* published an article on 'World Communications'. It warned that the future growth of the United States depended on the efficiency of US owned communications systems, just as Great Britain's had done in the past: 'Great Britain provides an unparalleled example of what a communications system means to a great nation standing athwart the globe . . .'. The ideology of the growth of communications, as represented in the mass media themselves, holds them, like Alice, to have 'just growed'. As *Fortune*'s warning demonstrates, they didn't.

Around the 1860s, the most progressive factions in the British ruling classes sensed how important it was to direct the growth of communications. Initially, the telegraph followed the spread of the railways. As modern industrialists themselves, the railway entrepreneurs employed the telegraph to improve their safety and control networks, also offering the service to private users. Soon, there were separate telegraph companies following the different routes of their big brothers, the individual railways companies.

However, there seems to have been a delay before it was generally understood that railways and the telegraph represent different types of infrastructure – the telegraph, though terrestrial, isn't a form of transport – and they were therefore destined to follow different patterns of capitalist development. The change in comprehension is recorded in legislation. During the 1860s, there were three Post Office Acts. The first, in 1863, merely defined the telegraph as a piece of wire. In the second, 1868, the Postmaster-General was empowered to 'acquire, maintain and work electric telegraphs'; the third, in 1869, amended the definition of the telegraph to include 'any apparatus for transmitting messages or other communications by means of electric signals'. This legislation, which effectively licensed a monopoly in an age which was deeply opposed to monopolies, was inspired by Gladstonian Liberalism – a political creed that was responsible for a series of expedient reforms in a number of fields, ranging from the disestablishment of the Church and the Education Act of 1870, to opening up higher civil service posts to examination and the 1872 Ballot Act.

If the case of the telegraph is a strikingly early example of nationalisation, the results were not encouraging. There have always been awkward contradictions in a statist undertaking of this nature. As in almost every example of social-democratic nationalisation ever since, the private companies were over-generously compensated to begin with, and the Post Office was unable to make the service run at a profit. A principal reason for this failure is the constitutional reluctance of the bourgeois state, having adopted nationalisation, to follow the appropriate logic and properly take care of investment. With this very first nationalisation, it also took time before the need for planning was understood. At the start it hardly seemed necessary: when it was nationalised, the telegraph system was still expanding, and for some time, all the Post Office had to do was go on opening telegraph offices all over the country (the number of telegrams sent in England and Wales grew from 7.1m in 1870 to ten times that number four decades later).

Incomprehension continued longer in the civil service than the Post Office itself, where new engineering concepts were gaining ground. However, the government's cost accountants, the Treasury, still thought in terms of the world of mechanical engineering, like bridge building and canal construction. When the telegraph had been invented, telegraphic messages, or telegrams, were at first regarded as apparently another form of mail, which is to say, a physical load, and this was still the spirit in which the 1869 Telegraph Act was drafted. When the telephone came along, and the Post Office wanted in, the definition needed to be stretched. They filed suit against the telephone companies under the terms of the 1869 Act, following the advice of government lawyers that telephone communications were telegrams within the meaning of the Act; and they proposed to the Treasury a plan for a comprehensive system of Post Office exchanges throughout the country. This the Treasury thought too expensive. The result was that while the GPO undertook a small number of local exchanges, more at first for business than for private use, much more important was the privately owned National Telephone Company, which grew by absorbing its other competitors. Not until 1912 did the Post Office take over the National Telephone Company and acquire a near monopoly of the whole system. (Meanwhile, the GPO had already become the largest single employee of middle-class women. By 1911, 14,328 women were engaged as telephonists and telephone operators, 20,337 as counter assistants or clerks.)

The establishment of the Post Office telegraph monopoly can be related to the progress of the newspapers and of Reuters. According to one commentator,

> The key to Reuters' dominant market position in the sale of international news to the British newspaper press was its relationship with the Press Association, the national news agency established by the provincial daily newspapers and formally constituted in 1868 . . . The Press Association adopted the task of disseminating national news to its member-clients, and also lent its support to the campaign for the nationalisation of the telegraph, which came about in 1870 (Boyd-Barrett, p. 113).

But Reuters' carefully nurtured ideology of objectivity was to come under challenge from the emergence before the end of the century of the yellow press, trading on a radically different set of news values, that came from the world of commercial entertainment rather than the boardroom. The creation of the yellow press debased improved intelligence in the same way traditional popular culture was debased in the growing commercialisation during the last twenty years of the century of music hall entertainment, with the formation of syndicates as the first step in the development of entertainment capital, with its own sectoral interests: what the Frankfurt School people in the 30s called the culture industry.

A profound shift in social sensibilities was involved in this process, which involved major changes in the structure of the press that deeply affected Reuters. The modern press evolved in two main stages: first, to service the needs of the capitalist and professional classes for organs of information, and then, as instruments directed to those social classes and strata over which the capitalist classes needed to extend their domination. The creation of Reuters belongs to the former, that of the yellow press (which appeared in the 1890s) to the latter. As rival agencies grew up to supply the needs of the new mass readership papers in the period leading up to the First World War, Reuters suffered declining profitability, from which it had only partially recovered when the Depression brought fresh financial deterioration.

The 30s produced another worry too: authoritarian currents in government began to talk of the advantages of something more

The Reuter Position Keeping Service installed in the Bank of America's Foreign Exchange Trading Centre in Los Angeles. The Bank says the installation is already allowing its dealers to increase transaction volume from a few hundred to thousands of trades a day with no paperwork and a 40% reduction in potential administrative errors.

than the kind of informal arrangements between the news agency and the State that came into operation during the First World war. The Fleet Street owners, the Newspaper Proprietors Association, found themselves persuaded to take joint ownership of Reuters alongside the PA. Later they were joined by various Commonwealth Press Associations, and further ownership links were created when Reuters became part owner together with the BBC and the television corporations of the white Commonwealth countries, of the world's foremost television news agency, Visnews.

VIII

The growing interaction of the scientific, the technical (or technological) and the financial (or economic) is clearly demonstrated in the way in which science was beginning in the 1860s to be integrated into the economic system through a number of new companies, the first purely scientific commercial enterprises, which manufactured the equipment for telegraph, cable and the telephone. The development of these companies had a chain of social effects. They created new professions, such as the electrical engineer. They provided what Bernal called 'the stock-in-trade for electrical experimentation – batteries, terminals, insulated wire (Faraday had to use wire from milliners or wind his own insulation), coils, switches, simple measuring instruments – and all at prices which even impoverished university laboratories could afford' (Bernal, p. 117). Soon these enterprises set up their own research departments, inventing a new business practice nowadays called r&d. The telegraph led directly to the telephone, and later to the wireless telegraph. It provided (Bernal again) 'a nursery for the young science of electromagnetism, supplying problems, part-time occupation, equipment and funds for the academic scientists and ensuring them plenty of students' (Bernal, p. 23). The telegraph and cable industries were also the sources of the new electric light, traction and power industries of the 1880s and 90s.

Bernal also makes the observation that the telegraph led to the addition of new electrical units of measurement to the age-old weights and measurements of trade and commerce. This is crucial. The telegraph was the first technology to establish information as a commodity, and therefore the need to measure it. Conceptually, this is the first step towards the modern distinction between hardware and software, and it belongs to the analysis of the peculiarities of the commodity form of all the electrical media, and later electronic media: including the telephone, phonographic recording, film, radio and television, which all got sucked into the same process. With each different medium you get new variants on the basic facts of technical linkage: if you've got something you can call software – the information you're passing around – then you've got to have something called hardware – the medium you pass it through.

This is reflected in the phenomenon of commodity linkage, which takes different forms, like cameras and film, or gramophones and records. Since you can't have one without the other, this gives rise to a general principle, namely, that manufacturers of any new kind of hardware have to concern themselves with the production of the appropriate software without which the hardware has no market. In this way, early producers of cinematograph equipment were also film producers and distributors – the very distinctions took time to appear. Or the early recording companies made both phonograph and phonogram; some still do. This can also be compared with the relationship between broadcasting and programmes. The first manufacturers of radios had set up radio stations *and* produced programmes, as a kind of loss leader, until the means were found to relieve them of the need, and institutional or commercial broadcasting began.

Observe that software becomes an ambiguous term here, on the one hand referring to the content which passes through the medium, on the other to the physical form which the content takes, the record on (or in) which the content is contained (or the modulated radio wave). Or it may not refer to the content at all. In the case of photography, the camera is no use without film, but you take your own pictures.

The ambiguity of the term software isn't just loose thinking; it comes from the fluid and shifting relationships between form and content which are characteristic of the media. Because the content of communication is symbolic, it is possible to translate it between forms in various ways, so that the different media become devoted to preying off each other: newspapers consume photographs, radio consumes records. In fact the relationship between the latter pair is thoroughly symbiotic. Radio needs records to help full up its air space, but the recording industry uses radio as an aural shopwindow to publicise and plug its ware.

These patterns relate to another series of peculiarities, in the commodity nature of the media, which have to do with the various different ways of consuming cultural products and therefore the different kinds of exchange value which are yielded. Thus, while cinema imitated the performing arts in collecting gate money – the cash paid in at the ticket window – and gramophone records imitated books, there were no pre-existing equivalent for broadcasting. The first manufacturers of radio not only had to produce programmes, they had to produce them gratis, because there was no way of selling them. Indeed, with the exception of pay-tv, programmes are still not exactly commodities from the point of view of the listener or viewer, but more like a right which comes with the purchase of the set, and in some countries, the payment of a licence fee. To finance broadcasting through a licence fee is one solution. Commercial broadcasting is another, which in the process creates another new kind of commodity: the airspace which is sold to sponsors and advertisers. It has even been said that the real commodity isn't the airspace, but people, the audience, according to the statistical breakdown of the consumer polls.

More recently still, in the case of video, there is a new upset, because the software already exists – on everyone's television set, in the same way as records and radio are fodder for tape recording. In the United States, the problems which this creates have reached the Supreme Court, in an action by Walt Disney against Sony for advertising videorecorders as a way of watching your favourite Disney programme whenever you want to. This alleged violation of Disney's copyright is a reminder that there are special kinds of property rights involved in this whole process. Copyright is a concept which has constantly shifted its meaning ever since it was first defined, in the wake of the invention of printing, to answer the question of the ownership of a text in terms of who held the right to make printed copies of written works – which at the beginning meant the printer-publisher, not the author. The history of copyright is the history of mounting contradictions in the legal superstructure, as the changing forms of cultural production altered the social relations of the author, who gradually became a new kind of intellectual worker (a shift which relatively few of them recognised until after Schiller and Marx). From the intellectual worker there has now descended the alienated mental worker whom Schiller and Marx foresaw; from the critical consciousness of the artist and the scientist, there have descended the programme producer and the computer programmer. Freelance programmers of all kinds, of course, still have an awkward tendency to organise themselves to claim the ancient privilege of copyright.

IX

This whole growing infrastructure has contributed independently to social relations by creating new sensibilities, new ways of relating to the world, and of representing it. Information is the lubricant of the capitalist mode of production, but at the same time it creates its own symbolic domain. If the human being is, as Merleau-Ponty said, condemned to meaning, then our mental existence cannot but reshape itself around the new languages and dialects which now occupy our world. We should think of this too as part of the Reuters Factor. It isn't just a question of information generating business, but of the nature of the information business itself, the way that gathering information treats the world.

For instance, the growing demand for information has created new metiers. Harold Perkin has suggested that statistics, which emerged as a discipline during the industrial revolution, 'is to industrialism what written language was to early civilisation: at once its product and its means of self-expression' (Perkin, p. 326). The Utilitarians, who promoted the Statistical Societies which exploded into activity in the 1830s, saw the role of statistics as, according to Perkin, the 'discovery and examination of "intolerable" facts, often long before they were felt to be intolerable by the press and public opinion'. But statistics also introduced the practice of surveillance, both commercial and bureaucratic. The kinds of information involved in this process come to impose their own terms of reference, which in turn become one of the ways in which capitalism represents itself to itself, seeming to impose order and reason where there is none.

X

The strategies adopted by the newspapers relate to their dual character, as organs of information on the one hand, and of influence on the other: their character, in other words, as synthetic forms of cultural production. This is entirely typical of the modern media, one might say symptomatic. It certainly helps to explain how social susceptibilities are shaped in ways that people aren't normally consciously aware of. The social unconscious is formed of many elements, reaching back through the diverse heritage of popular culture as well as the impact on traditional belief of the successive shocks of social 'progress'. The influences which shaped the character of the mass press in Britain include, for example, such features of popular culture as the broadsheet ballads and the art of the patterer, which had both served for the dissemination of news.

The traditions of popular culture were sustained through the development of new forms of popular entertainment, like music hall. To begin with, musical entertainment was subjected to progressive commercialisation without any help from new communications technologies until almost the end of the century. Then, the phonograph, which first appeared in 1877, introduced another peculiarity: it was primarily a cultural phenomenon, which did little to increase the circulation of information – on account of which, it was much slower to develop into a major branch of capital. Its connection with the complex of modern scientific-based industry is amply shown by its birth in Edison's research laboratory, but for several decades it seemed to lead a more or less independent existence as a minor branch of the entertainments industry, and was only recapitalised and reconverted with the development of electrical recording in the 1920s, after the invention of electronic amplification during the First World War.

The phonograph brought about a cultural revolution in the interim nonetheless. At the beginning, after the invention of the first mechanical means of sound recording by Edison in 1877, economic exploitation was impeded simply because there was no mechanism for duplication of the recording. The early cylinder machines made good side-shows in the fairgrounds, and they had the attraction for the private purchaser that you could make and show off recordings in the home, but this hardly provided a mass market – much more restricted, for example, than the telephone, which was also sold, in its early years, as a luxury item for the home.

But the phonograph added nothing to the communications apparatus, because it didn't carry information; its improvement was therefore less urgent, and didn't attract the same investment funds as other new instruments. That is why its massification had to wait thirty years. The industry only took off after Emile Berliner accomplished a series of improvements during the course of the 1890s, culminating in the first wax disc recording in 1900. The wax disc served as a master for a copper matrix from which copies could be made. Now there opened up a new and enormous market. Its nature can be judged from a trade advertisement put out by the New York-based Victor Company in 1905, with photographs of leading recording artists and a text which explained: 'Three show pictures of operatic artists, one shows pictures of popular artists. Three to one – our business is just the other way, and more, too; *but there is good advertising in grand opera .*' The gramophone now began to do for music what telegraphy had done for information: it created new conventional forms, both standardised and truncated, extended the reach of the market, and increased circulation.

Again the Reuters Factor was at work. The record found a much larger audience than the artiste could reach in person in theatre or concert hall, both in terms of numbers and of geographical extent, and before long the record industry took on an international character. Music has always travelled – people carry it with them – but now began a process of wholesale trade which transplanted music from one place to another whatever the cultural predilections and differences. It also overrode the musical cultures it penetrated by imposing its own increasingly industrial nature, which Adorno in particular has analysed, seeing it as a process of fetishisation of musical characteristics in a way that negates their aesthetic authenticity. The result has been to transform the social role and functions of music. In 1967 a Mr Joseph Klapper of CBS was able to tell a US Congressional Committee, inquiring into 'Modern Communications and Foreign Policy', that 'the broadcasting of popular music is not likely to have any immediate effect on the audience's political attitude, but this kind of communication nevertheless provides a sort of entryway of Western ideas and Western concepts, even though these concepts may not be explicitly and completely stated at any one particular moment in the communication' (Schiller, p. 106).

XI

For all this to happen, however, the gramophone needed the radio. The case of Guglielmo Marconi and the invention of radio is another example of how the interest of the military in improving their communications systems comes to be of crucial importance at the earliest stages of development of a new communications technology. Marconi, like similar pioneers, had been able to achieve primitive wireless transmission over short distances as a very young man working at home with his father's resources, by 1895. But then he needed financial support on a considerable scale. When the Italian navy turned him down, he found the support he needed in England, where his mother came from, and his family connections were the right ones. He rapidly had the Post Office, the War Office and the Admiralty all involved in the development of the invention.

Important early steps for commercial wireless telegraphy included the first ship-reporting service which Marconi supplied for Lloyd's of London in 1898, and in the same year, the first journalistic use, when the Dublin *Daily Express* decided upon a publicity scheme and used the wireless to report the Kingstown Regatta. Two years earlier, when Marconi arrived in London, was a key year in the development of mass communications and mass entertainment in England, the year of the first cinematograph shows and the birth of Alfred Harmsworth's new *Daily Mail*. Marconi made skilful use of newspapers as a medium of publicity in promoting his invention on both sides of the Atlantic, and they were eager enough to be used. New inventions were a great source of public wonder, and even better, of circulation. The latest scientific wonders were showmen's acts. The man the English claim as the inventor of cinematography, William Friese-Greene, who didn't do too well with his invention, was reduced to treading the boards demonstrating the incredible new x-rays. This is extremely ironic when you consider that music hall was the perfect launchpad for the film – together with the fairground and the tradition of the travelling showman – and that once films took off, they slowly strangled their host.

It was the cinema, more than any previous invention of new communications technology, which suddenly changed the ground-rules. Film was from the very beginning peculiar in two things: it established itself first with the mass audience, and only then filtered upwards through society. This can be compared with the immediately preceding inventions of the telephone and the phonograph. Both of them found their first markets within the bourgeoisie and only later became working class commodities. You can see this in the earliest publicity announcements for the telephone, which spoke of business needs first, of its social usefulness second, and of its value as a personal luxury item third. In the case of the gramophone, as Berliner renamed it, its initial appeal was also found among social groups with special cultural interests, since even after discs first appeared, the period of primitive pre-electrical technology in the industry was protracted: with the lack of improvement, the original spontaneous fascination of the populace slackened, and it helped to be able to keep a market of immigrants in New York happy with recordings of Italian opera.

But film had no such problems. Its appeal was not only immediate and huge, but all such cultural differences were submerged in it. The fact that its characteristics were primarily aesthetic, and it added to the apparatus of commercial intelligence no more than the gramophone, hardly mattered in the face of its rate of growth. Because of this, and because no country in which film appeared was capable of producing enough to supply the market, film was also international from the outset; by the time of the First World War, it had begun to attract the interest of finance capital. It was the equivalent in the sphere of cultural production to the transnational character of the electricity industry, which Lenin held to be ushering in imperialism – the highest stage of capitalism.

XII

We have surveyed the nineteenth century and what do we find? First, that the growth of industrial capitalism, and indeed, of imperialism, is intimately linked with the invention and development of new means of communication. It is a process in which military interests play a significant role, though not always as central as in the twentieth century, the epoch of neo-colonialism. The needs of commercial intelligence, however – in other words, of the bourgeois class itself – are constantly very much to the fore and provide the initial markets. Here is a parallel with the Thatcherite approach: Thatcherism looks to the application of the new high-tech in the form most beneficial to corporate capitalism itself. A rationale results: to achieve this application, corporate capitalism must be free to do whatever it wants to.

In the nineteenth century, the new communications begin to form a new infrastructure, which stands, however, in contradiction with the ideology of entrepreneurial capitalism, principally because it needs state regulation and control if the piecemeal initiatives of individual entrepreneurs are to be effectively welded together. Hence we find the first steps in international co-operation designed to establish certain basic universal standards, but in each new branch of communications there is a bitter fight between capitalist competitors before the victors are able to establish technical standardisation. This is, of course, extremely wasteful. Yet in the Thatcherite vision of the coming of high-tech, there is to be the same chaos in the marketplace, the same destructive wastefulness.

We also saw that this new infrastructure progressively opened up new economic opportunities for the exploitation of cultural production. For example, alongside the commercialisation of popular entertainment like the music hall, and the creation of the first mass readership markets, the 1880s saw the hugely successful introduction of the Kodak camera – "You press the button, we do the rest", which made photography the first new popular art form of modern times. As the century draws to a close, the pace of innovation accelerates. Photography waited forty years for its massification. The delay in the case of the phonograph is less than thirty; and by this time, cinematography has burst upon the world. In the course of these developments we find a distinction growing up between communications technologies where the primary function is the transmission of intelligence which has a practical or instrumental use value, and those where the content is primarily symbolic – which are primarily, in other words, new means and media of cultural production and reproduction. Both, however, operate in certain respects in curiously similar ways. In both cases, there is a necessary distinction between what is later called hardware and software, though to be sure, each technology has its own peculiarities (just as the products of different media have different peculiarities as commodities, in the way they realize their exchange value).

The development of electronics during and after the First World War radically modifies the separation between different media and reshapes the entire communications industry. With radio, talkies and television, there emerges a culture industry in which all branches of communication are implicated, and in which intelligence and information plays second fiddle to the universal levelling of mass consumption. Their function – most starkly seen in the United States – is not to produce an informed and educated population, with a higher cultural level, but to shape their consciousness to the needs of increasing passive consumption, in which the products of the media themselves consume a greater and greater proportion of consumer spending. Thus the economic development of the media – involving, as always, the multiplication effect of the Reuters Factor – extends and intensifies still further both the information network and their own cultural net. To this is now being added the impact of microelectronics, which is profoundly contradictory.

The progressive enhancement of potential cultural production brings inevitable new contradictions. As Hans Magnus Enzensberger observed fifteen years ago, it is wrong to regard the media merely as means of mass consumption. They are always, in principle, also means of production. The contradiction between producers and consumers in the mass media is not inherent but institutional, and it has constantly had to be reinforced by economic and administrative measures (including the appropriate design of the equipment itself). But the original massification of photography was precisely a matter of placing a new cheap means of cultural production into the hands of the masses. Such an enterprise can be very risky; it had been necessary to repress a radical press that appeared during the industrial revolution, and to seek to control the self-education movements which the new industrial proletariat had created. Yet although photography, then 16 and 8mm cine, and now computers, are accompanied by their own sub-industries devoted to the culture of the amateur, there have repeatedly been eager users who fall beyond the pale, and create alternative uses and networks of users. It is to the defence of alternatives at every level that the critique of Thatcherism must be directed.

Many commentators have observed that it is a misnomer to speak of the communications media: the media are used to prevent communication. But this is precisely because what Brecht said of radio in 1932 not only remains true, but in the age of microelectronics and the computer, and the promise of 'interactive information/entertainment', becomes even more pertinent:

> Radio must be changed from a means of distribution to a means of communication. Radio would be the most wonderful means of communication imaginable in public life, a huge linked system – that is to say, it would be such if it were capable not only of transmitting but of receiving, of allowing the listener not only to hear but to speak, and did not isolate the listener but brought about contact. Unrealizable in this social system, realizable in another, these proposals, which are, after all, only the natural consequences of technical development, help towards the propagation and shaping of that *other* system . . . If you should think this is Utopian, then I would ask you to consider why it is Utopian.
>
> Brecht, *Theory of Radio* (1932)

References

J.D. Bernal, *Science and Industry in the Nineteenth Century*, Routledge & Kegan Paul, 1970.

Oliver Boyd-Barrett, *The International News Agencies*, Constable, 1980.

Hans Magnus Enzensberger, 'Constituenmts of a Theory of the Media', in *Raids and Reconstructions*, Pluto, 1976.

Karl Marx, *Capital* I, Lawrence & Wishart, 1970.

Harold Perkin, *The Origins of Modern British Society 1780–1880*, Routledge & Kegan Paul, 1972.

Herbert Schiller, *Mass Communication and American Empire*, Boston, Beacon Press, 1971.

Graham Storey, *Reuters' Century*, Max Parrish, 1951.

'World Communications', *Fortune*, May 1944.

'E.T.':
Technology and Masculinity

David Albury

Zanussi – the appliance of science

Brainstorm: it started as research – it ended as nightmare.

These two advertising slogans need little decoding since they encapsulate so precisely the ambiguities present in dominant popular representations of science and technology. Whether it be within fictional forms (the horror movie, the T.V. sci-fi adventure, the novel of scientific discovery) or 'factual' forms (*Horizon, Tomorrow's World*, the endless stream of books and articles on the 'micro-revolution'), the images of science and technology are constructed in such a way that a mixture of awe and fear, respect and distrust are engendered in the audience. 'Zanussi – the appliance of science': expert knowledge applied to the problems of human welfare. 'Brainstorm: it started as research, it ended as nightmare': the scientist dabbling with evil forces, Faustian man:

These necromantic books are heavenly,
Lines, circles, scenes, letters and characters:
Ay, these are those that Faustus most desires.
Oh, what a world of profit and delight,
Of power, of honour, of omnipotence,
Is promised to the studious artisan!
All things that move between the quiet poles
Shall be at my command.
-Faustus

Oh help us heaven! here art Faustus'·limbs,
All torn asunder by the hand of death.
The devils whom Faustus served have torn him thus.
-Scholars[1]

But Faustus sets a trend in more ways than one; through the lineage of Goethe, Shelley and R.L. Stevenson we arrive at the horror films of this century. These films ('House of Terror', 'The Walking Dead', 'Frankenstein', 'Dr. Jekyll and Mr. Hyde') are one of the most popular genres of film. Together with their television counterparts, they provide a large section of the 'public' with an influential, consistent picture of the scientist, albeit one which exaggerates certain characteristics (eccentricity, dedication to the pursuit of knowledge/power, financial independence).

But these fractured; contradictory images of science do indeed represent realities of science and technology. Antibiotics, telephones, relativity theory, space travel, PVC and the structure of DNA all inspire awe and respect for the improvements they bring to (many of) our lives and the understanding they give us of 'the world around us'. But chloracne, asbestos, nuclear holocaust, thalidomide and technological unemployment crowd in to create the fear and distrust of the scientific enterprise. New theories, new technologies, the man in the white coat, the computer and the test-tube: any of these symbols in isolation is pregnant with the potentialities of progress and destruction. Placed in contexts, their meanings are often rendered unambiguous: the nightmarish washing machine is not a possibility.

These emotions of fright and wonder are, of course, two sides of the same coin of mystification. The socially-created ignorance of the dynamics and constructedness of the artefacts of science and technology leave the mass of the population in no position to analyse or evaluate the reasons for the development of the latest theory in physics or the newest miracle drug or to predict the consequences of the introduction of foetal surgery or the application of neo-Darwinian theory. The labour process of science and technology is so effectively hidden, or displayed as a unidirectional path to advancement and truth pursued by the lone heroic genius, that all we – now those labelled as 'scientifically illiterate' – can do is to gaze upon these explanations and objects that may as well have come from outer space (a favourite theme of the science fiction genre).

On the 'rational' plane, this mixture of emotions is often resolved into the 'pure' science/nasty technology dichotomy. This is a view not confined to the TV or cinema audience but regurgitated constantly by academic historians and sociologists of science. This neutralist attitude towards science renders its content immune from socio-political comment and criticism whilst displacing people's anxieties onto the technologists and appliers of scientific knowledge or leaving the anxieties unresolved as the failure to adjust to 'progress' (change). The use/abuse model of the science, technology and society relationship, of which this model is a variant, has been much criticised;[2] here I do not wish to add to the criticism but wish merely to point to the emotional structures within which the model operates.

The emotions and the pleasures which people experience through the representation of science and technology are far more complex than the stark poles I have so far indicated. For example, it is by no means clear, at least to me, whether it is *theories* of 'nature' or nature itself which people are awed by: think of the many 'natural history' programmes where the lingering awe at the *technique* of the production replaces both science and nature as the focus of attention. However, although the response to these representations is far from non-emotional, there is a sense in which the 'rational' activities of science and technology expect and receive a 'rational' response. Although the breathless admiration for the latest product of twentieth-century capitalism suffuses BBC television's *Tomorrow's World*, the programme is (presumably) aiming to explain and demystify so that we can rationally appreciate how socially and intellectually beneficial the product is or (more usually) will be.

HOW MANY TIMES

HAVE YOU SEEN *E.T.* ?

With the exception of 'natural history' slots, science programmes, like science itself, attract a disproportionately male audience. *Tomorrow's World*, the one deviant from this pattern, has a more family audience (and a clean, wholesome 'family' of male and female presenters) but this is undoubtedly due in large part to its scheduling between *Dr. Who* (or in earlier series, *Nationwide*) and *Top of the Pops*. The presentation within the programmes reflects the rationalistic, objectivistic approach of science and technology, ensuring that any emotional responses remain securely enclosed behind the mask of masculinity.

It is only in the relatively recent past that this 'mask of masculinity' has become an object of academic or political scrutiny. Feminism and the women's liberation movement re-initiated and urged an analysis and critique of genderisation and sexuality within the context of the heady revolutionary years of the late '60s and early '70s in the post-swinging cities of Western Europe and North America. Foucault's *History of Sexuality*[3] attempted to demolish the dead-end dyad of 'repression' and 'liberation' and replace it with a description of the constructedness of some of our innermost feelings.

Post-Foucauldian writers have foregrounded pleasure/desire within socio-political analyses and prompted and reflected the drift towards therapy of semi-disillusioned middle-class radicals.[4] All this has made it respectable once again for socialists and feminists to read psycho-analysis in their search for a richer, deeper form of politics. However, these tendencies, which fit well with the politics of despair and the failure of mass politics, have produced few analyses which take masculinity as their central problematic. In one sense, recent feminist and non-feminist work in this area has reproduced female sexuality as the problem area and male sexuality as the 'given'. (In some radical feminist writing male sexuality is not only 'given' but 'natural'.) I believe that an analysis of 'E.T.' allows us to make a contribution to our understanding of masculinity and, *inter alia*, of its linkages with technology and technological choice.

'E.T.' –the Audience

I first saw 'E.T.' by accident. I set out with a friend to see 'Gandhi', which had just opened, in search of an evening's entertainment and political enlightenment. 'Gandhi' was booked out. 'E.T.' was showing at the cinema opposite and so, believing we would at least be enthralled by the special effects, we joined the queue. As we waited, the people behind us recounted the number of times they had seen 'E.T.' (5 in one case, 3 in another). 'Crazy', I thought, especially as they were adults, and I had categorized 'E.T.' as a children's film – the type of movie I generally feel I need the excuse of an accompanying child to see.

I came out of the cinema completely disillusioned, burning with a lump in my throat, tears in my eyes and on my cheeks, and with a desire to see the film again as soon as possible. I was clearly not alone. As the handkerchieves and kleenex were deployed I realised that this piece of celluloid had achieved a remarkable feat.

Grown, adult men were crying (so indeed were many women, but in my experience this is not so eventful). What was it that had so moved these men? What was it that had 'released' this socially disapproved-of behaviour? What was it that had so effectively pierced the 'mask of masculinity'?

Since that initial viewing I have seen 'E.T.' another half-dozen times. I know few men who have seen the film without being affected. Of course, there are male behaviours which quickly re-seal the 'mask' – sullenness, the boisterous invitation to the pub, or the excessive, compensatory machismo. I have endlessly questioned and bored relatives, friends and acquaintances – both children and adults. The vast majority of boys, especially younger ones, are massively engaged by the film; even months later they are able to recount and re-enact long scene-by-scene sequences.

The female responses are more highly differentiated. Many girls have experienced the film as 'silly', 'stupid' or overly sentimental; attitudes reiterated by some adult women who see it as peculiarly male (a view with which I agree and shall argue below), if touching in parts. On the other hand, a considerable number of females have given a more positive valuation and been as deeply engrossed by various themes of the film as men and boys.

By tracing the themes of technology, masculinity and their relationship in the film, I hope to provide some explanation of this highly differentiated and unusual audience 'reaction'.[5] By doing this I will also be answering those questions that are more conventionally asked of films. Why was[6] this film (and its by-products) a blockbuster success? (The trite answer of 'good marketing' seems insufficient, as well-marketed products not infrequently flop). Why did people, in different ways, experience/construct pleasure in this film? How do we (some of us) come to like such a grotesque figure as E.T.?

'E.T.' – the Film

Although primacy is given to the child-adult relationship in the film, as will be seen below, many other social and psychological cross-cutting divisions and conflicts are dealt with. Strong representations of male/female, state/individual, technology/nature and, of course, not forgetting, extra-terrestrial (E.T.)/terrestrial relationships pervade the film. Indeed many early criticisms revolved around the way the film collapses the integrity and autonomy of these divisions into the child-adult conflict, especially in the climactic moment of E.T.'s 'death'.[7]

The opening scene and much of the movie is shot from a child's, often Elliott's, eye position. A spaceship has landed on earth and its occupants are carefully gathering plant specimens. While we do not clearly see the occupants, there is no doubt of their immediate empathy and one-ness with flora and fauna. Thus is established their ecological sensitivity and their technological sophistication of interstellar travel. Gradually the area around the spaceship is encircled with pickup trucks, and the spaceship departs. But in the hurry to get away, it leaves behind one of its occupants. Large men get out of black vehicles and with flashing lights, belts weighted with guns and jangling keys begin to search the forest for the creature which remains. The motives of the men are transparent – surveillance, capture, jailing. In the darkness, all we see is the lower half of male adults trampling the undergrowth both scared of and scaring the unidentified 'thing' – a thing which emits a soft light and a high-pitched yell. Frightened and frightening, the creature evades capture and gazes out over the illuminated ground plan of a US town.

Elliott (the living embodiment of E.T.), the other central character, is the middle child of a broken home. Nine or ten years old, he has an elder brother (Michael) and a younger sister (Gertie) who live with their mother, whose name (Mary) is fleetingly mentioned, in a typical American suburban middle class home. The father, whose recent separation is upsetting the mother, is stated to be in Mexico with his lover, Sally.

Michael is entertaining some friends at home and they send Elliott out to get a pizza. On his return he hears something in the garden shed, approaches, throws a ball into the shed. The ball is thrown back; he catches a glimpse of E.T., freaks and runs screaming back into the house. E.T. flees back to the forest. His brother and friends rush out to the shed clutching knives and full of bravado but find nothing. Despite his insistence, all Elliott's family disbelieve his story, with the sister and the brother pouring scorn on his tale and accusing him of imagining dinosaurs, dragons and other fairy-tale monsters. Elliott, in a prophetic statement, says 'Dad would believe me.'

The next day Elliott decides to meet E.T. and sets off for the forest, where he lays a trail of sweets. E.T., it transpires, follows the trail back to the garden. That night Elliott, scared but entranced, creeps into the garden and, for the first time gets a fairly good look at E.T. – a dwarfed foetus-like creature with extending neck, long arms, spindly fingers, wizened face and bulging eyes. By means of more sweets, Elliott leads E.T. into his room and, exhausted by excitement, falls asleep. The following morning Elliott feigns illness to stay off school and learn more of his newly-acquired friend, pet or toy.

He shows E.T. the things in his room, naming them for him and explaining their function. He feeds E.T. on some choice products of US agribusiness. When Elliott cuts himself, E.T. extends his magical, illuminated finger and heals the wound.[8] And when Elliott points and identifies parts of his face, E.T. points to his equivalent feature.

Michael returns home early and – after being forced to swear an oath to his brother, 'You have absolute power' – is introduced to E.T. Amazed and frightened, with Michael's disbelief dispelled, the brothers hear their mother and sister come in. Gertie rushes upstairs, into Elliott's room, sees E.T., starts to scream and is shut up by Michael putting his hand over her mouth. Eventually Gertie quietens down and asks whether E.T. is a girl or a boy. 'A boy, of course', Elliott resolutely replies. And as the fear dissipates, Elliott tries to establish deeper contact with E.T.

A map is produced, Elliott points to his home town and asks E.T. where his home is. E.T. is bewildered. A globe is found, Elliott indicates the United States and again asks E.T., 'Home?' E.T. points out of the window. The children don't understand. E.T. then gathers together various spherical objects and, in a moment of sheer magic, invests them with movement so that they circle in the air in the form of an orrery. E.T., the prize possession of Elliott, has thus demonstrated power over both animate and inanimate matter. Through E.T. Elliott has mastery over material objects and nature. Fascination, enchantment, emotion and power are bound together in (in fact, form) the relationship between Elliott and E.T.

The day after, Elliott, leaving E.T. safely in his toy cupboard, goes to school. There follows a series of scenes in which the relationship becomes one of (or is demonstrated to be) not that of friendship but of identity. E.T. leaves Elliott's room, waddles downstairs into the kitchen, opens the fridge and helps himself to some cans of beer. The film cuts back and forth from E.T. at home to Elliott at school. As E.T. gets drunk, so we see Elliott becoming woosy. When E.T. bumps into something, Elliott is hurt and rubs his head. E.T. gets drunker and Elliott slips down his chair. E.T. accidentally switches on the television, gazes in wonder and Elliott experiences the emotions of the characters on the screen.

Elliott is in the middle of a biology lesson, where each child in the class is given a frog in a jar. The (male) teacher, again only the lower part of him is seen, moves from pupil to pupil popping a cotton wool ball impregnated with chloroform into the jars. At this time E.T. is looking at a cartoon strip of a science-fiction adventure where an extra-terrestrial being is using a radio to contact his home to escape from earth. E.T. is thinking about how to return to his own kind. Elliott rushes round the class tipping over the jars to let the frogs escape – in the process causing a generalised panic, in the middle of which, in the final moment of identification, as E.T. watches a classic Hollywood kiss on the television, Elliott seizes one of the girls in the class and enacts the very same kiss. There is no doubt that E.T. and Elliott are as one. This identification is reinforced many times later in the film, especially when Elliott litters his conversation with 'we think', 'we are', 'we know' and Michael says to Elliott 'What's all this "we" stuff?'

With E.T. still careering around the house drunk, Elliott's mother and Gertie come into the house. The mother does not see E.T. even though he is in front of her eyes, even when she knocks E.T. over with the fridge door and despite her daughter's attempts to tell her about E.T. Elliott's school phones and his mother goes off to fetch him. Gertie takes the opportunity to befriend E.T. In the course of pointing out letters and objects in the room and on the TV, she realises that E.T. is croaking words back to her. Gertie, a female, gives the power of language to E.T. When the brothers arrive home they find an E.T. (who to the horror of Elliott has been dressed up in little girl's clothes) who can communicate. Echoing the cartoon strip he has seen earlier and Gertie's later instruction, E.T. persistently says 'E.T. phone home, E.T. phone home.' (As the Bell Telephone Company in the USA says, 'Home is only a phone call away.')

Under the guidance and supervision of E.T., Elliott and Michael look for various objects in the garage so that a transmitter can be constructed. A saw blade, an umbrella, an old radio, components of a broken-up Texas Instruments 'Speak and Spell' and other bits and pieces discarded by their father (and hence evoking memories of him) are collected and taken into the house. Using the excuse of Halloween fancy dress the brothers smuggle E.T. out of the house and back to the clearing in the forest where E.T. landed.[9] Here E.T. assembles a Heath Robinsonish radio and begins sending signals to his compatriots. But no response is received and Michael goes home leaving E.T. and Elliott still tryir ;. Elliott falls asleep and then in the morning awakes to find E.T. ias disappeared.

Meanwhile, Elliott's mother is going frantic as to what has happened to her son. The police are called and, as the search is about to start, Elliott comes into the house tired, ill, dejected and depressed. Whilst being scolded and cared for, Elliott implores Michael to go and find E.T. After some frantic searching, Michael discovers E.T. cold, grey, crumpled and lifelessly lying on some stones at the edge of a stream. He takes E.T. home. Michael asks Elliott what is wrong. 'We're sick. I think we're dying', Elliott replies. So desperate are he and Elliott as to E.T.'s state that they solicit the help of their mother. She is shocked, horrified and paralysed by E.T.

Interspersed through all the above have been scenes of black vans, bristling with aerials and other symbols of high technology – even of 'national security' – cruising around Elliott and Elliott's home trying to monitor, track down and capture E.T. And as the family and E.T. are together, with Elliott and E.T. ill, the agents of surveillance invade. The previous images of shadowy men and dark vans become transformed into brilliant white. The house is enclosed in a massive plastic bubble fed with air through a huge plastic tube. Men in white suits emblazened with stars and stripes enter and convert the living room into a gigantic high-tech operating theatre. Outside white police cars with flashing lights and lorryloads of equipment assemble. Elliott and E.T. are placed on adjoining operating tables and strapped into the paraphernalia of modern medicine. Medicine, the state, the police, science and technology – the adult male world – envelop the home, the family, Elliott and E.T.

The traces of the ECG brain scans, pulse, blood pressure and breathing are all monitored: E.T. and Elliott are completely in synchronisation. Michael is quizzed by a doctor. 'Elliott thinks his thoughts?' 'No', Michael replies, 'Elliott thinks his feelings.' The senior surgeon tries to comfort Elliott, 'He came to me too. I've been waiting for this since I was 10 years old.' But the aim of the medical apparatus is to sever the link between Elliott and E.T. despite Elliott's protestations 'E.T. Stay with me, please. Stay together. I'll be right here. Stay. Stay. Stay.' Medicine wins, the traces begin to diverge and the doctors announce in triumph, 'They're separating, they're separating.'

E.T.'s traces move to the familiar and doom-laden continuous horizontal while Elliott regains normality. The surgeon attempts to console Elliott: 'What do you feel?' 'I can't feel anything anymore', Elliott replies. Elliott is left alone with E.T., who is now being preserved in an ultra-cold vessel. Elliott, with tears streaming down his face, lifts the lid to say his farewell, gazes at E.T., whispers 'I *love* you' and E.T.'s heart begins to glow and his body to revive. E.T. starts to speak, Elliott yelps with excitement and drops the lid to stop the chattering E.T. from being heard by anyone else. While continuing to feign grief, Elliott relates his good fortune to Michael and together they engineer E.T. in his vessel into a van which they drive off to escape. Attached to the van is the vast white birth canal which previously pumped air into the house. clinging to the end of the tube are two men in their white, flagged space suits trying to recapture Elliott and E.T. Elliott releases the tube and with the help of some friends they transfer E.T. from the van to the basket of a bicycle ridden by Elliott and head for the forest.

In true children's film tradition there ensues a chase. Elliott and E.T. on one bicycle accompanied by Elliott's friends on others with police cars and vans in hot pursuit. A road block is formed, rifles are readied and at the crucial moment E.T. lifts the entire troupe into the air, over the heads of the bewildered men and onto the clearing in the forest. On their way the bicycle with Elliott and E.T. upon it passes in front of the moon, re-enacting the publicised image from *Mary Poppins* as a reinforcement of this as being a child's fantasy.

In the clearing, E.T.'s spaceship lands and the farewell scene takes place. The family is re-united (mother, daughter, sons and father[10]). With choked-back tears and stiff upper lip, Michael shakes hands with E.T., Gertie says a tearful goodbye and gets a patronising 'Be good' from E.T., and Elliott steps forward. 'Come', beckons E.T. towards the spaceship. 'Stay', says Elliott. 'Ouch', says E.T., and then, extending his magic finger towards Elliott's forehead, 'I'll be right here.'

E.T., Elliott's fantasy, ascends the steps of the spaceship and stands in the entrance as the jaws, the gates, close in front of him sealing the fantasy as the craft rises into the sky. The fantasy is gone but the fantasy remains.

No wonder this film appeals to and engages men. The audience is constructed and identified as male. The central and active characters are male; the positions that women occupy, and are therefore offered, are marginal and subordinate – a weak, chaotic (if caring) mother, a screaming sister who wishes to dress E.T. as a doll. The film is the story of the male fantasy. E.T., as that fantasy, is enchantment, emotion and *power*. In the film, this fantasy becomes repressed and expressed in the adult male as an alienated, unfeeling power manifested in disenchanted and disenchanting technology; real power, but at the cost of emotion and love.

In 'E.T.' this dramatic representation of masculinity – the technology/power/repression triplet, is contrasted against the more enchanting, magical, ecological 'technology' and outlook of E.T. Although I have mentioned the ecological sensitivity of E.T. in the above, I have not given it the weight it has in the film. In the opening sequence of the film, while animals flee from the marauding adults, a rabbit is shown unaffected by the presence of the extra-terrestrials. Elliott's family dog shows no fear of E.T. When E.T. is present, plants flourish and grow; as E.T. becomes ill and 'dies', plants wither. Indeed E.T.'s illness is undoubtedly attributable to the alien and despoiled climate on earth where no real life can be sustained. And when he is found by Michael, he resembles a dead fish washed up on the banks of a polluted river.

Spielberg himself has said: 'The main threat is the fact perhaps that this creature cannot live too long in this environment. It's the atmosphere, the air, the biology, the chemistry, beware-of-the-water, whatever . . .'[11] An empathetic, non-exploitative understanding of nature which heals cuts and can construct utility out of the discarded junk of capitalism stands beside and in opposition to a Weltanschaung that tramples on feeling in its quest for measurement and removes sensibility from our appropriation of the cosmos. Within this framework we can comprehend why the adult male world finds the fantasy so threatening, why it needs to capture E.T. This is not, as so many critics have argued, to recapture a lost childish innocence but to *contain* an alternative world-view. A world-view which respects feeling and pain (E.T. can stop Elliott's tears with a touch of his magic finger) and does not submit emotion to a 'technological imperative'.

Lest I be misunderstood, the centrality of power in the male (child and adult) fantasy is not innate or inherent but deeply constructed. I reject the notion of a *natural* masculinity. To return to an introductory point, 'E.T.' displays what all too many science-fiction and children's films lack – an appreciation that science and technology are not given, inevitable entities but series of negotiated and constructed choices. These choices moreover are not made merely within social, political and economic contexts but are also profoundly rooted in psychic and emotional structures.[12] To remake science and technology, to make a radical science and technology, we must remake life at the 'personal' as well as the 'political' level.

'E.T.' is a film about what happens to fantasy and emotion in the emergence of the male child into adulthood. Michael's friends have sneered at Elliott's 'belief' in E.T. in the beginning, and are masculinely loitering outside Elliott's house during the 'illness' wearing masks of gangsters, cowboys and other male stereotypes.

They are then stunned back into feeling and rip off their 'masks of masculinity' when confronted by E.T. – the fantasy locked within them all. Power over nature, technology, can take many forms, of which 'our' technology is but one. 'E.T.' should be seen for the clarity with which it exposes the articulation of the constructed power-orientation of male fantasy with the different forms that technology can take: a more entertaining treatise on 'choice of technology' than policy-makers generally recommend.

'E.T.' - the Footnote

Many reviews (*Sight and Sound*, *Screen*, *New Musical Express*) have drawn attention to the religious parallels that pervade the film. Most explicitly, E.T. as the symbol and provider of life, health, goodness and miracles undergoes death and resurrection.[13] In my view this religiosity operates on two levels. Religious structures, particularly Christianity, provide a conventional and popularly understood framework for Spielberg to work within. Our reading the film into a religious context is a way of giving meaning to the themes that we, as the audience, detect.

But these levels mask an underlying unifying structure. God, technology and E.T. are all forms in which the alienation of people from nature is expressed. All are seen as inhuman, supernatural and extra-terrestrial. The alienation of deistic religion was, of course, analysed by Marx and needs no rehearsal here.[14] E.T. is extra-terrestrial and, quite explicitly, Elliott's alienated fantasy power. Science and technology as forms of alienation have received explicit discussion, not least in the work of Sohn-Rethel.[15] Thus to read 'E.T.' as a re-telling of the traditional Christian story misses the possibility of thinking about the questions it poses for an understanding and practice of science and technology. 'E.T.' itself represents technology and machines as alienated. As the cars draw up at the beginning of the film, there is no sight of any driver, just the headlights casting their beam across the countryside. The machines are depersonalised and inhuman. 'Tron', which appeared at the same time as 'E.T.', is premised on technology as alienation by being set in two imaginary worlds: the world of the 'users' and that of the 'programs'. Its story is the attempt of a 'user' to recapture the world of the 'programs', the alienated products of the 'users'. Where 'Tron' suffers in comparison with 'E.T.' is in its counterposing of the 'virtues' of masculinity (strength, courage and rationality) rather than offering an alternative theorisation and practice, as 'E.T.' does.

'E.T.' – the Conclusion

At the beginning of this review, I drew attention to the profoundly contradictory experiences and feelings that people have of science and technology. Awe and fear lie side by side in the popular consciousness and are evoked in the film by a (perhaps over-simple) resolution into an awe-inspiring, innocent, empathetic power over the world and a terrifying destructive, exploitative and oppressive technology. The subversive moment of 'E.T.' resides in its reinforcement of the distrust of the state and technology, but it offers a fairly conventional solution in the respect for the mystical and the magical. The science/masculinity relationship is explored and deconstructed – only to be recomposed with a traditional dichotomisation of the masculine and the feminine on the terrain of childhood innocence. It is no surprise that Spielberg's next film is to be *Peter Pan*.

Indeed, the whole film and especially the final scene can be viewed as an exploration of separation. When E.T. and Elliott embrace before departure, Elliott's gaze oscillates between the manifestation of his power-fantasy (E.T.) and the security of his mother in his questioning, or the questioning for us, of the possibility of a third way – an adult life bereft of 'innocence' but non-oppressive.

> Believe it or not, I never thought 'E.T.' would be a big commercial success. I thought it was my first personal movie, and I did not know it would be as infectious as it turned out to be.[16]

Spielberg's naivety/innocence, demonstrated in this quote, has clearly and consciously been a motivating factor in much of his work. In a recent radio interview, he recounts how his fascination with the extra-terrestrial started in childhood when he lay on his back with his father in a field, looking at a meteor shower. An experience he described as intoxicating and full of 'wonderment' and which led to his 'wondering if there are people out there like me or my parents'. His first film, and many of his subsequent films, represents the alien and the extra-terrestrial as friendly and good – in deliberate opposition to the dominant representations of them as hostile, a set of representations he sees as a reflection of the cold war nerves of the late 1950s and early 1960s. How easily this naivety can be captured within existing forms of society and technology can be seen by Spielberg himself applying to be one of NASA's first shuttle civilian passengers in order further to expand his 'naive sense of wonder'. Anthony Holden, the radio interviewer, unsurprisingly concludes by asking, 'Are you a little boy who has never grown up?' 'I have and I haven't . . . I have remained naive', Spielberg replies.

Acknowledgements

I would like to thank members of the Radical Science Collective and Alan O'Shea for useful comments and criticisms on an earlier draft. Also I would like to thank Pauline Jackson for several ideas as well as for her research efforts in procuring a copy of the 'E.T.' Exhibitors Campaign Book.

Notes

1. From Christopher Marlowe's *Dr. Faustus*, Act 1 Scene 1 and Act 5 Scene 3.
2. See, e.g., B. Young: 'Science *is* Social Relations', *Radical Science Journal*, 5 (1977), 65-129. D. Albury, J. Schwartz, *Partial Progress*, Pluto, 1982. M. Hales, *Science or Society*, Pan, 1982.
3. M. Foucault, *The History of Sexuality, Vol. 1: An Introduction*, Penguin, 1981.
4. See, e.g., S. Heath, *The Sexual Fix*, Macmillan, 1982. S. Cartledge, J. Ryan, eds., *Sex and Love*, Women's Press, 1983. A. Snitow et al., eds., *Desire*, Virago, 1984. R. Coward, *Female Desire*, Paladin, 1984.
5. It cannot of course be stressed strongly enough that this research on audience 'reaction' is highly impressionistic and operated on a totally non-random sample. the 'proper' research is yet to be done (ESRC take note).

6. 'Was' rather than 'is' because 'E.T.' has been withdrawn by its distributors, no doubt as the second phase of its well-planned marketing strategy: the creation of expectation. Before its first release (I would guess pre-Christmas 1984 for its second) it was impossible to get sequences for view – unlike many other films which, if you watch Barry Norman, trailers, etc. you can see virtually all of before the première.

7. 'E.T.' was directed by Steven Spielberg, among whose other films are *Jaws* and *Close Encounters of the Third Kind*.

8. This scene deeply imprints on many, especially male, children – perhaps not surprisingly, since a common behaviour of friendship among young children is the mutual introduction to one another's prized possessions.

9. As will become clearer after reading through the entire article, this scene has considerable significance. Partying and fancy dress are traditionally 'legitimate' contexts in which fantasies can 'escape', be expressed, made public.

10. Despite my several viewings of the film, it is still not obvious to me that the present adult male is actually the father. I think it may be the surgeon. Or perhaps the surgeon is the father!

11. *E.T. the Extra-Terrestrial*, Exhibitors Campaign Book, 1982, p. 6.

12. In case people think I am thus relegating social, political and economic determinants, see my and Joe Schwartz's *Partial Progress*, which bends the stick in the other direction.

13. Other noted religious parallels include the mother's name (Mary) and E.T., robed in white, leading the disciples (the bicycle-riding friends) out of danger.

14. There is, however, no succinct précis by Marx of his analysis. The intrepid can wade through *The Holy Father* and *Capital*, Vol. 1, Chapter 1, Section 4.

15. For an introduction see his 'Science as Alienated Consciousness', *Radical Science Journal*, 2/3 (1975), 65-101; reprinted in *Radical Science* (RSJ reprints), Free Association Books, 1985.

16. Steven Spielberg interview in *Sunday Times* 3 June 1984.

CSP•
CRITICAL SOCIAL POLICY

a journal of socialist theory and practice in social welfare

ISSUE 10 SUMMER 1984

A theory of human needs
LEN DOYAL AND IAN GOUGH

Community Policing: towards the local police state
PAUL GORDON

Mobilisation without emancipation?
Women's interests, state and revolution in Nicaragua
MAXINE MOLYNEUX

Struggles in the welfare state
Mental health in Nicaragua

Contracting out in the NHS

Commentary on social policy
Towards the unitary state: Tory attacks on local government

The GLC
PHIL BLACKBURN

The Metropolitan County Councils
ROGER FELLOWS AND KEITH GRIMES

The Personal Social Services
CAROL O'BRIEN

The 'backlash in' family law: the Matrimonial and Family Proceedings Bill
JULIA BROPHY

Reviews

SUBSCRIPTION RATES

	U.K.	Overseas Surface	Overseas Airmail
Individuals	£7.00	£9.00 US$15	£14.00 US$22
Insitutional	£19.00	£22.00	£28.00
Students & Unwaged	£5.00		

Single Issues and Back Numbers (please specify)

	U.K.	Overseas Surface	Overseas Airmail
Individuals	£3.00	£4.00	£5.00
Institutional	£6.00	£8.00	£10.00
Students & Unwaged	£2.00		

Orders for single issues or subscriptions to be sent to: Judith De Witt, Business Manager, CSP, 46, Elfort Road, London N5. Cheques payable to 'Critical Social Policy'. Trade orders to Pluto Press, 105(a) Torriano Avenue, London NW5 2RX.

NEWS & NOTES

1984 CONFERENCE OF
RADICAL SCIENCE PERIODICALS

Les Levidow

'Sympathy for the Devil'

This year's gathering was, again, held in two parts – a public conference, followed by a private meeting over Easter weekend – both parts well-organised by the *WechselWirkung* collective in Berlin. Although 'Traditional and Alternative Applications of Computer Technology' was the formal theme, 'Sympathy for the Devil' became a central metaphor for expressing our ambivalence towards computers. Large publicity posters – featuring the 'devil' slogan in day-glo colours – were put up all over town, especially the underground platforms, and further publicity came from a press conference and radio interviews.

This year, more than ever before, the participating journals defined the political content of the public conference. The all-day (April 20) plenary session was held in a Technical University lecture hall filled with about two hundred people and revolved around five presentations, each followed by discussion:

Bob Young (Radical Science Collective), 'How Do Technologies Embody Values?';

Les Levidow (Radical Science Collective), 'Economic Planning and Left Strategies';

Angelo Dina (*Scienza Espérienza*), 'New Technologies and Workers' Strategy';

Julius Thaler (Wuseltronick), 'A Different Kind of Technology Production'; and

Tom Athanasiou (*Processed World*), 'The Community Memory Project'.

As the full proceedings of the plenary session are available elsewhere,[1] this report will simply mention the themes that the speakers took up. Bob Young's talk posed the question of how we could enhance oppositional uses of new technologies by embodying anti-capitalist values in their design. He elaborated upon the 'pipeline' metaphor for describing how capitalist values normally get embodied – yet also how subversives could intervene in the process of setting the social priorities in technological origination at the beginning of the pipeline, when the design and use criteria get decided. In the discussion, one person invented the slogan, 'Make the pipeline leaky!'.

Les Levidow, who was asked at short notice to emphasise the Lucas Aerospace episode, located the Lucas workers' defeat within the larger contradiction between alternative technology and the capitalist market. His other examples came from shopfloor struggles over the control of automation, and from initiatives of the Greater London Enterprise Board. The discussion revealed how many people had held illusions about a mythical workers' victory at Lucas or tended to evaluate the experience solely in terms of alternative products.

Angelo Dina's talk described in detail the anti-worker design of new technologies at FIAT. He proposed intervening to minimise their negative effects at the application and design stages, rather than attempt to obstruct them outright. His strategic proposals followed on from his fascinating account of how management's designs for automation achieve both more domination and less disaffection among the workers that remain.

photos: WechselWirkung

Next Julius Thaler described the experience of the Wusel-tronick Collective (from 'wuseln', to fiddle around) in designing socially useful products through collective discussion and decision-making. Although computers were not initially central to the group's work, it was decided to use them despite reservations, especially about which tasks should be computerised.

That kind of project came under at least implicit criticism from Tom Athanasiou, who criticised 'hi-tech alternativism' for reinforcing ideologies of technological progress. His talk described attempts by the Community Memory project in Berkeley to design an 'electronic bulletin board' that people could use to define 'communities of interest', in opposition to the normal use of computers for commodity-exchange or mere leisure. His account of Pacific Software, a firm that some CM members set up to subsidise CM, showed how it predictably encountered its own contradictions in the capitalist marketplace for software.

On the second day of the public conference, about 60 people attended small workshop discussions. These took up some contradictions of the alternative use of computers, even outside of capitalist firms: for example, the experience of computers often seemed to make the 'user' (drug metaphor intended) feel closed off from other people, and it created standards of perfection that made the typewriter seem too primitive to use at all. Do word processors devalue other ways of writing, even talking? Does their over-prescription hide the real problems? A progressive-sounding example was a French government project to develop a small, solar-powered computer for use by nurses in the Third World to analyse patients' symptoms and recommend treatment – even though few of them would be able to get hold of the drugs that the computer might recommend.

Another problem raised was how to overcome divisions between R&D workers and other workers who could usefully learn from the former about management's plans against them. In practice R&D workers will rarely act against their short-term class interests by siding with other workers against management. And the workers about to be further disciplined, or even replaced, often don't want to know, preferring to think: 'It won't be me.'

Journals Meeting

The weekend meeting was held at a lovely lakeside resort run by a workers' welfare organisation outside Berlin. Participating journals included *Radical Science, WechselWirkung (WW), Revoluon, Scienza Esperienza, Science for the People* and two newcomers: *Terminal 19/84* and *Processed World*. We had introductions from those two and updates from others:

Terminal 19/84, which started publishing in 1980, came out of oppositional conferences on infotech. Through the membership-based Centre d'Information et d'Initiative sur l'Informatisation

photo: WechselWirkung

(CIII), the magazine is able to sustain a circulation of 2000 copies, including 500 subs, and support a paid worker; its editorial collective consists of about fifteen computer professionals, all men. Although the magazine is mainly about computers, it has a broader appeal as France's only radical science periodical, and it has come to include more social theory than at its beginning. It gained special notoriety upon publishing a self-interview, really a letter, from the 'Committee for the Liquidation and Subversion of Computers', better known by its French acronym CLODO' (see No. 16, October 1983; reprinted in *Processed World* No. 10). No police retaliation followed, though computer security firms have cited the letter to justify the need for their products.

Processed World, 'the magazine with a bad attitude', started off based on disaffected (though highly paid) computer workers and high-tech clerical workers in California's Bay Area. The collective sees the magazine's humorously anti-authoritarian, anti-work approach as appealing to many potential subversives who would otherwise be missed by the left. The magazine is unusual for encompassing the various divisions of labour – janitors, secretaries, computer programmers – and in linking struggles against work discipline to wider cultural questions.

Scienza Esperienza – whose acronym, *se*, means 'if' – was launched in 1983. It has succeeded in selling 12,000 copies per issue, almost all through bookshops and newsagents, which are required to carry such periodicals. It has taken up debates on mental institutions and new technologies in the home and office. In apparent contradiction with its serious journal-type articles, it uses a tabloid format with outlandish graphics – often unrelated to the articles, yet thematic within each issue and attracting a readership in their own right. The editorial group came largely out of *Sapere*, which now resembles more conventional 'popular science' magazines.

Saturday afternoon's session took up some general problems facing all the journals. Even if a journal is able to finance a full-time paid worker, that role risks preventing full participation by the collective members. Yet it's difficult to do without such a worker, especially since the journals have had less voluntary labour available to them recently. Another general problem is the difficulty of maintaining contact with what scientific workers do, even though the journals are not necessarily aimed at them in particular.

We went on to discuss new forms of struggle resulting from new technologies. Everyone acknowledged that, for example, robotised assembly lines are less easily disruptable than traditional ones. However, Angelo Dina argued that nevertheless we shouldn't always defend the latter, since there are possibilities for transforming robotised lines by making them dependent upon new skills that capital doesn't want but can be forced to accept; such a victory could bring better working conditions. Similarly he thought it futile to oppose office automation and proposed instead a fight to reduce the control aspect of new technologies there.

In our discussion, others pointed out that such automation leads to a staff reduction which in turn helps management to select the most obedient workers to keep on. Also, *WW* members pointed out that industrial workers in West Germany feel intimidated by the threat of foreign competition, which management uses to win acceptance of automation and/or worse working conditions. Most workers fear losing their incomes, more than losing their boring jobs as such, while trade unions tend to judge success by the number of jobs retained, rather than by the type of jobs or the income retained by workers and unemployed workers. After some discussion of union proposals to do a 'deal' with capital for the sake of 'saving jobs', we felt it made no sense to propose any kind of deal or alternative within the constraints of the profit-system (as is being promoted by sections of the Left, especially in the USA and Britain). It remained unclear how an opposition could win implementation of pro-worker designs for new technology if they ran against the interests of profitability.

Journal Projects

Sunday morning's session began with a *Terminal 19/84* proposal to publish an international collection of material on 'the police use of computers and against liberty'. Our discussion pointed to some political limitations of such an approach, as compared to one locating the problem within the class struggle. In practice it's less meaningful to cite violations of individual civil liberties than to analyse state strategies against its potential enemies, on whom it systematically collects information. Examples from the UK include the General Kitson-style 'low-intensity operations' on Northern Ireland's nationalist (Republican) population; the mass arrests, surveillance and interrogation of striking miners; Neighbourhood Watch schemes organised by the police in the name of 'crime prevention'; and as-yet unsuccessful attempts to do 'race checks' on black people claiming unemployment benefits or using National Health Service hospitals, in the name of catching out immigrants and visitors ineligible for such benefits and free services.

What's needed is a way to overcome people's sense of fatalism over new technologies which apparently give the state invincible powers through information. So it's worth noting that, in all the examples mentioned above, the state's power is not primarily dependent upon computers. Rather, collection of the information itself requires an exercise of power which can be resisted.

Next we discussed *Revoluon*'s plans for a special issue on the role of science in rearmament and possible conversion to non-military production; the journal collective said they are keen to interest people in 'post-Cruise' issues before the present peace movement in Holland dissolves. For scientists in particular, we thought it necessary to undermine their justifications for doing military-funded projects – be it an overtly pro-military ideology of 'peace through strength', or the more subtle illusion that their research can't possibly benefit the military. Of course, almost any research has some potential military use, so it's not enough to distinguish among different kinds of research according to their funding source. Rather than simply point a finger at those research projects or industries specifically geared to military purposes, we thought it necessary to see how the war industry affects the development of science and industry as a whole – for example, through promoting the model of the 'paper-free, worker-free' factory. Contributions to this critical project are welcome.[2]

Sunday evening we briefly discussed campaigns needing our attention. *SftP* reported on a suppressed attempt to found a radical science periodical in Israel (see Postscript). We reported on the case of Geof Sirockin, whom Queen's University, Belfast, was threatening to dismiss in retaliation for his exposé of health hazards both in the University and in the Divis Flats, a nationalist housing estate in West Belfast. Also, Dhirendra Sharma – a contributor to our No. 14, *No Clear Reason* – had been suddenly transferred from the Centre for Studies in Science Policy by J. Nehru University, in response to his exposés of India's nuclear programme. Lastly, *se* reported on a campaign to stop the Italian government from repealing legislation that had stipulated the closure of mental institutions. The proposed repeal reflected the failure of the earlier reform to provide adequate facilities for the patients being deinstitutionalised, so it's not enough simply to oppose the repeal.

Sunday evening's session concluded with a discussion of green or ecology parties. This was mainly to take up the issues raised by the forthcoming (May 1984) conference involving members of West Germany's Green Party, ecological institutes and the *WW* collective. Among the latter there were different views on the purpose of the conference: to improve the Green Party's policies? to sharpen debate with *WW*'s own readers (most of whom vote Green)? to use them for campaigns that needed parliamentary manoeuvres? For example, it was proposed that the Green Party initiate bills against automation and against Personnel Information Systems (see *Processed World* 9, pp. 40-47), so as to add publicity to struggles already going on. The proposal was made despite disagreement with the Greens' decision to go parliamentary, since that move seemed to have displaced direct action groups formerly active on environmental issues.

Examples from other countries suggested fewer possibilities for using green parties there than in West Germany. In France the Ecology Party isn't seen as representing an ecology movement anyway, and it has even promoted the myth of personal home computers as offering a 'clean' ecological solution to the present crisis. In Italy, although some ecologists understand the consequences of capitalist development, they remain overenthusiastic about particular 'alternative' solutions within capitalism. In the USA, the case of Burlington, Vermont was cited as an example of how environmentalist pressure groups declined after the election victory of a socialist mayor, who then sold them out to business interests. There wasn't much to say about 'green party' activities in Britain, where the Ecology Party seems a ragbag of disparate interest-groups with little radical (much less subversive) consciousness. In all these countries, it remains unclear whether the parliamentary direction causes the problem or merely highlights already-existing limitations in environmentalist movements.

The final session on Monday morning decided to plan the 1985 public conference on the theme of biotechnology. Some of us had reservations about choosing that theme, given that biotechnology seemed far removed from our own practice and from the possibility of a left alternative (unlike, for example, computers). Yet we felt there was some possibility for mobilising popular demands for biotechnology to take a different direction than at present – if only to illustrate how biotechnology now embodies the values of capitalism, the further commodification of social relations (e.g. surrogate mothers, spare body parts). Of course, even without the obvious evils of capitalism, biotechnology would still raise difficult philosophical and ethical questions about the nature of life, what it means to be a human being. To resolve the ethical quandary, some critics propose a total moratorium or even 'taboo' on tampering with the nucleus of the cell, though many of us saw this as evading the question of an anti-capitalist ethics.

Postscript on Israel

In 1980 the Israeli authorities refused permission for Dr. Najwa Makhoul to publish an Arabic-language journal intended to explore technology and society from a Marxist and feminist perspective, applying the idea of a 'science for the people'. When the government received a petition of protest from an international array of signatories, they received a reply from Itzhak Shamir, then Attorney General, who said that in this case 'state security reasons outweighed freedom of the press'. In 1983 a second application from Dr. Makhoul was also rejected.

Israel has strict censorship laws, and even some anti-Zionist periodicals have been granted licences, so there is some mystery as to why Dr. Makhoul was not permitted to publish a single issue of her proposed journal. She has since said,

> Had I not been a Palestinian Arab scientist and woman, and the license had not been for a scientific publication in Arabic, I would probably not have been denied the right to publish. These are the only features which actually distinguish my project from ones which were granted licenses . . . Security risk claims were mobilized precisely to

stop me from exercising my right to publish. [The real aim] is not to permit Palestinian Arab scientists to create forms of meaningful existence here and consequently to [get] them to leave the country and discourage those abroad from returning home.

Perhaps it is [the presence] and the return of Palestinian Arab intellectuals who are citizens of the Jewish state that constitutes in itself a security risk?

Dr. Makhoul had already run into conflict with the authorities on other occasions: in attempting to organise the first national meeting of Arab citizens of Israel – banned; and in helping to coordinate the first public opinion polls in the occupied territories – only to be threatened with imprisonment if she published her findings. Since then the Hebrew University has decided not to renew her contract as lecturer there.

For more information, see the articles listed below. To exchange critical material with Dr. Makhoul, write to her at the newly-formed Jerusalem Institute for the Study of Society, 6 Bnai-Brith Street, Jerusalem 95146, Tel. 226-916.

Stop Press:
Inaugural International Conference on
'SCIENCE AND THE EXIGENCIES OF POLITICS'
Jerusalem   31 August–4 September 1985

Details from: **Jerusalem Institute For The Study of Society**
6 Bnai-Brith Street, Jerusalem 95146, Telephone: 226-916

Nat Hentoff, 'Is It Because I'm an Arab, a Woman or a Scientist?', *The Village Voice*, 20 March 1984, p. 8.

Gary Keenan, 'Would Science for the People Be Banned in Israel?', *Science for the People*, March/April 1984, pp. 5-6.

William McPherson, 'Israel Deals with a "Security Risk"', *The Washington Post*, 13 March 1984.

Notes

1. The pre-published papers are available in English from the Radical Science Collective for £6 photocopying and postage costs; they include 'Electronic Data Processing: An Alternative to Taylorism' by Carlos Derbez and Guy Lacroix, two members of the *Terminal 19/84* collective who were unable to attend the conference. Two of the talks delivered (by Levidow and Athanasiou) were very different from the prepared texts, so we are offering to make copies of our cassette tapes of the day's proceedings, including the discussion: £5 for the set of 3 tapes. Also, a version of Athanasiou's talk is published in this volume.

2. Send material to Revoluon, Postbus 1328, 6501 BH Nijmegen, Holland. Also, a Critical Bibliography is being prepared by Bruno Vitale, 8 rue des Bugnons, CH 1217 Meyrin, Switzerland.

INFOTECH AS CLASS DECOMPOSITION

Autonomie — Materials Against the Social Factory

We have learned that you are interested in the *Autonomie* issue on new technology (no. 13) and had asked for a summary. Before I do the summary, let me say something about the context of no. 13. This issue is part of a major project entitled 'Imperialism and the Future of Work in the 1980s'. In this context, we have published an issue on Imperialism/anti-Imperialism, another one on labour markets, and a third one on capital's technological offensive.

We analyse the present trend of social policy and work reorganisation as a response to workers' struggles of the early 1970s. For the metropolitan centres, the organisation of a series of international crises (food, oil, debt) means the contraction of investment, segmentation of the labour market, and social policy as a means of disorganising and 'decomposing' the working class. We examine the new technologies in this context: computer sciences and their applications, in production, as a new stage of Taylorising work but at the same time realising the capitalist dream of abolishing the working class as a political factor. In the content of state control, this means a new form of the state, replacing Keynesian forms of institutionalised mediation with algorithms of power: domination of the working class through computerised planning, and pauperisation mediated by social policy.

The first article, 'Sabotage', examines workers' attitudes to machinery in different historical phases and movements: Luddism, in the context of the 'moral economy' of the pre-industrial crowd; syndicalism and the forms of industrial unionism which accepted machinery as the basis of struggle for a craft workers' culture, or which, as newly industrialised/proletarianised strata, attacked machinery as a form of resistance, and the international cycle of struggles in the automobile sector in the early 1970s, involving sabotage and refusal of work itself on the assembly line. Then the article discusses the possibilities of sabotage of the new forms of information technologies, which require a 'scientific' form of sabotage, as well as attacks from outside the workplace because the working class within the workplace is being profoundly decomposed.

The second article, 'Information Technology, a New Stage in Class Struggle', is a more philosophical text. It poses the question of how far the introduction of cybernetic machines introduces a new level of class struggle, not only as a new Taylorism, but as a qualitatively new stage: while the mechanical stage was the doubling of the forces of nature ('Verdopplung der Naturkräfte' — Marx), the new stage is the doubling of reality (Verdopplung der Realität). The violence and disruption imposed on the working class today, decomposing it, would be comparable in impact to the violence that machinery imposed on the pre-industrial masses. The article briefly discusses the consequences for the marxist problem of value. Then it concentrates on two aspects: the genesis of a new role of the state; and the new relationship of perception (Erkenntnis), individual and social constitution, and class struggle. On the one hand, it analyses how social reality — as a living, creative process — is being replaced by the information network of the state; this analysis includes a historical retrospect on the Nazi-era census. On the other hand, it points out that 'information work' precludes a world-view antagonistic to the established order, because the object of perception and the process of perception turn out to be identical. It follows that the destruction of information technology is a precondition of social/ individual reconstruction.

The next article, 'The Data-Offensive of Social Policy', analyses the collection of personal data as a form of 'real subsumption' of society as a whole. The conclusion of this article is different from the first two: it envisages a new class subjectivity opposed to data-projects. Another article, 'On the Modernisation of the Planning Machinery of the State', points out further aspects of the state's cybernetic model as regards the planning process as a closure of social mediation and antagonism. The article, 'On the Way to Complex Automation, Tendencies in Management and Organisation of Labour' points out the role of the chip and of decentralised numerical control on the production line, as regards the decentralisation of the factory and the segmentation of labour. There follow analyses of Volkswagen's policy and transnational structure, of the struggles at Alfa Romeo, an interview with Benjamin Coriat on the 'Post-Taylorist Factory System' (reprinted from *Liberation*), a report on a struggle in a small woodworking factory, and a brief report from a prisoner about a high-security prison and forced labour.

Correspondence to: Autonomie, c/o Dr. med. Eberhard Jungfer Friedrichstr. 21, D-2000 Hamburg 4, West Germany.
Orders to: Autonomie, c/o Thadenstr. 130a, D-2000 Hamburg 50; single copy price DM 14, payable in DM only.

CONNECTIONS

PUBLICATIONS RECEIVED AND NOTICED
Published in London unless otherwise noted.

Nicholas Abercrombie, Stephen Hill, Bryan S. Turner, *The Dominant Ideology Thesis*, Allen & Unwin, 1980, Pp. x + 212, pb.

Karl Abraham, *Selected Papers on Psycho-Analysis* (1927), Maresfield Reprints, 1979, Pp. 527, hb £10.00

S.H. Adams, *Modern Sewage Disposal and Hygienics*, E. & F.N. Spon Ltd., 1930, Pp. x + 473, hb.

Ziggi Alexander and Audrey Dewjee, eds, *Wonderful Adventures of Mrs Seacole in Many Lands*, Bristol, Falling Wall Press, 1984, Pp. 247, pb £3.95

Frank Arkwright, *The ABC of Technocracy*, Hamish Hamilton, 1933, Pp. 96, hb.

Ronald Aronson, *The Dialectics of Disaster: A Preface to Hope*, 1983, Pp. xi + 329, pb £5.95.

Inge Bates, John Clarke, Philip Cohen, Dan Finn, Robert Moore and Paul Willis, *Schooling for the Dole?: The New Vocationalism*, Macmillan, 1984, Pp. vii + 236, hb £20.00, pb £6.95.

Marshall Berman, *All That Is Solid Melts Into Air: The Experience of Modernity*, Verso, Pp. 384, hb £18.50, pb £5.95.

Lynda Birke and Jonathan Silvertown, eds., *More Than the Parts: Biology and Politics*, Pluto Press, 1984, Pp. iv + 268, pb £7.95.

P.M.S. Blackett, *Atomic Weapons and East–West Relations*, Cambridge University Press, 1956, Pp. vi + 107, hb.

Robert Boakes, *From Darwin to Behaviourism: Psychology and the Minds of Animals*, Cambridge University Press, 1984, Pp. xiv + 279, hb £35.00, pb £15.00

Derek Bok, *Beyond the Ivory Tower: Social Responsibilities of the Modern University*, Harvard University Press, 1984, pb $7.95.

Tom Bottomore, *The Frankfurt School*, Tavistock Publications Ltd., 1984, Pp. 93, hb £7.95, pb £3.25.

Charles Boyle, Peter Wheale, Brian Surgess, *People, Science and Technology: A Guide to Advanced Industrial Society*, Brighton, Harvester Press, 1984, Pp. xii + 265, pb £5.95.

Wilmette Brown, *Black Women and the Peace Movement*, Bristol, Falling Wall Press, 1984, Pp. 92, pb £2.95.

Sue Cartledge and Joanna Ryan, *Sex and Love: New Thoughts on Old Contradictions*, The Women's Press, 1983, Pp. 237, pb £4.95.

Jeremy Charfas, *Peer Commentary on Peer Review: Case Study in Scientific Quality Control*, Cambridge University Press, Pp. 71, £6.95.

Andy Chetley, *The Crisis in Infant Feeding*, War on Want, 1981, Pp. 31, pb 75p.

Alice Cook, Arlene Kaplan Daniels and Val R. Lorwin, eds., *Women and Trade Unions in Eleven Industrialized Countries*, Philadelphia, Temple University Press, 1984, Pp. xiii + 327, hb $34.95.

Helen & Peter Cooper, *Heads or the Art of Phrenology:* London Phrenology Co. Ltd., 1983, Pp. ix + 105, pb £5.95.

Mark Cousins and Athar Hussain, *Michel Foucault*, Macmillan, 1984, Pp. vii + 278, pb £6.95.

D.P. Crook, *Benjamin Kidd: Portrait of a Social Darwinist*, Cambridge University Press, 1984, Pp. vii + 460, £30.00.

Descartes, René, *Discourse on Method and the Meditations*, Penguin, 1968, Pp. 188, pb £1.75.

Ilham Dilman, *Freud and Human Nature*, Oxford, Basil Blackwell, 1983, Pp. vi + 207, £15.00.

Ilham Dilman, *Freud and the Mind*, Oxford, Basil Blackwell, 1984, Pp. vi + 204, £15.00.

Harold Evans, *Good Times, Bad Times*, Coronet Books, Hodder and Stoughton, 1983, Pp. 525, pb £2.95.

John Fekete, ed., *The Structural Allegory: Reconstructive Encounters with the New French Thought*, Theory and History of Literature, Vol. II, Manchester University Press, 1984, Pp. xxiv + 269, pb £9.50.

John Forrester, *Language and the Origins of Psychoanalysis*, Macmillan, 1980, Pp. xvi + 285.

Ronald Frazer, *In Search of a Past: Autobiography*, Verso, 1984, Pb.

David Frisby, *Georg Simmel*, Ellis Horwood/Tavistock, 1984, Pp. 161, pb £3.25.

Erich Fromm, *On Disobedience and Other Essays*, Routledge & Kegan Paul, 1984, Pp. vii + 148, pb £5.95.

Ann Game & Rosemary Pringle, *Gender at Work*, Pluto Press, 1983, Pp. 147, pb £3.95.

Peter Gay, *The Bourgeois Experience: Victoria to Freud, Volume 1, Education of the Senses*, Oxford University Press, hb £18.50.

John E. Gedo, *Portraits of the Artist: Psychoanalysis of Creativity and its Vicissitudes*, NY, The Guilford Press, 1983, Pp. 303, hb.

Michael Gibbons and Philip Gummett, eds., *Science, Technology and Society Today*, Manchester University Press, 1984, Pp. 198, pb £4.50.

Sander L. Gilman, *Seeing the Insane*, New York, Chichester, John Wiley & Sons, 1982, Pp. xiii + 241, £42.50.

Jonathan Glover, *What Sort of People Should There Be?: Genetic Engineering, Brain Control and Their Impact on Our Future World*, Pelican, 1984, Pp. 190, pb £2.50.

Malcolm Haslam, *The Real World of the Surrealists*, Weidenfeld and Nicolson, 1978, Pp. 264, hb £12.50.

Larry Hirschhorn, *Beyond Mechanization: Work and Technology in a Postindustrial Age*, Cambridge, Mass., The MIT Press, 1984, Pp. viii + 187, £16.60.

Rainer-W. Hoffman, *Arbeitskampf im Arbeitsalltag: Formen, Perspektiven und gewerkschaftspolitische Probleme des verdeckten industriellen Konflikts*, Frankfurt, Campus Verlag, 1981, Pp. 156, pb DM 28.

Donald Horne, *The Great Museum: The Re-Presentation of History*, Pluto, 1984, Pp. v + 265, pb £5.50.

Julian Huxley, *Soviet Genetics and World Science: Lysenko and the Meaning of Heredity*, Chatto and Windus, 1949, Pp. x + 245, hb.

Martin Ince, *Sizewell Report: What Happened at the Inquiry?*, Pluto, 1984, Pp. 212, pb £3.95.

Douglas Kellner, *Herbert Marcuse and the Crisis of Marxism*, Macmillan, 1984, Pp. xii + 505, hb £22.50, pb £8.95.

David Kettler, Volker Meja, Nico Stehr, *Karl Mannheim*, Ellis Horwood/Tavistock, 1984, Pp. 169, pb £3.25.

Michael Kidron & Ronald Segal, *The New State of the World Atlas*, Pan, 1984, Pp. 170, pb £6.95.

Jack Kloppenburg and Martin Kenney, 'Biotechnology, Seeds and the Restructuring of Agriculture', *Insurgent Sociologist*, *12*, 3 (Summer 1984), 3–17.

Karin D. Knorr-Cetina and Michael Mulkay, *Science Observed: Perspectives on the Social Study of Science*, Sage, 1983, Pp. 272, pb.

Robin Tolmach Lakoff and Raquel L. Scherr, *Face Value: The Politics of Beauty*, Routledge & Kegan Paul, 1984, Pp. viii + 312.

Christopher Lasch, *Haven in a Heartless World: The Family Besieged*, Basic Books, 1976, Pp. xvii + 230, $4.95.

Christopher Lasch, *The Minimal Self: Psychic Survival in Troubled Times*, New York, W.W. Norton, 1984, Pp. 317, $16.95.

Peter Leonard, *Personality and Ideology: Towards a Materialist Understanding of the Individual*, Macmillan, 1984, Pp. xii + 228, pb £5.95.

Angela Livingstone, *Lou Andreas-Salome*, Gordon Fraser, 1984, Pp. 255, £18.50.

Joseph Lopreato, *Human Nature & Biocultural Evolution:*, Allen & Unwin, 1984, Pp. 350, hb $24.95.

S.E. Luria, *A Slot Machine, A Broken Test Tube: An Autobiography*, Harper & Row, 1984, Pp. x + 229, £12.50.

Jean-Francois Lyotard, *The Postmodern Condition: A Report on Knowledge*, Manchester University Press, Theory and History of Literature, Vol. 10, 1984, Pp. xxv + 110, hb £23.00, pb £7.50.

Angela McRobbie and Mica Nava, eds., *Gender and Generation*, Macmillan, 1984, Pp. xii + 228, hb £15.00, pb £5.95.

Joanna Rogers Macy, *Despair and Personal Power in the Nuclear Age*, Philadelphia, New Society Publishers, 1983, Pp. x + 178, pb $8.95.

Nicholas Maxwell, *From Knowledge to Wisdom: A Revolution in the Aims and Methods of Science*, Oxford, Basil Blackwell, 1984, Pp. vi + 298, £19.50.

Dianna Melrose, *Bitter Pills: Medicines and the Third World Poor*, Oxford, Oxfam, 1982, Pp. 277, pb £4.95.

Jeannette Mitchell, *What Is to Be Done About Illness and Health?*, Penguin, 1984, Pp. 300, pb £2.95.

Sean Murphy, Alastair Hay, Steven Rose, *No Fire No Thunder: The Threat of Chemical and Biological Weapons*, Pluto, 1984, Pp. 145, pb £3.95.

Dorothy Nelkin and Michael S. Brown, *Workers at Risk: Voices from the Workplace*, London, The University of Chicago Press, 1984, Pp. xvii + 220, £17.00.

David F. Noble, *Forces of Production: A Social History of Industrial Automation*, New York, Alfred A. Knopf, 1984, Pp. xviii + 409, $22.95.

Dorinda Outram, *Georges Cuvier: Vocation, Science and Authority in Post-Revolutionary France*, Manchester University Press, 1984, Pp. viii + 299, £25.00.

Arnold Pacey, *The Culture of Technology*, Oxford, Basil Blackwell, 1983, Pp. viii + 210, £15.00.

Paul Piccone, *Italian Marxism*, London, University of California Press, 1983, Pp. xii + 206, £19.95.

Robert B. Reich, *The Next American Frontier*, Penguin, 1983, Pp. 324, pb £2.95.

Yvonne Roberts, *Man Enough: Men of 35 Speak Out*, Chatto & Windus, 1984, Pp. 308, pb £4.95.

Joan Rothschild, ed., *Machina Ex Dea: Feminist Perspectives on Technology*, Oxford, Pergamon Press, 1983, Pp. 264, hb £18.00, pb £7.15.

Ziauddin Sardar, *The Touch of Midas: Science, Values and Environment in Islam and the West*, Manchester University Press, 1984, Pp. x + 253, £20.00.

Calvin O. Schrag, *Radical Reflection and the Origin of the Human Sciences*, Indiana, Purdue University Press, Pp. 146, pb $4.50.

Barbara Seaman and Gideon Seaman, *Women and the Crisis in Sex Hormones*, Brighton, Harvester Press, 1978, Pp. viii + 502, £12.50.

Michael Shallis, *The Silicon Idol: The Micro Revolution and Its Social Implications*, Oxford University Press, 1984, Pp. vii + 188, £8.95.

Peter Singer & Deane Wells, *The Reproduction Revolution: New Ways of Making Babies*, Oxford University Press, 1984, Pp. viii + 273, pb £2.95.

Gareth Stedman Jones, *Language of Class: Studies in English Working Class History 1832-1982*, Cambridge University Press, hb £22.50, pb £6.95.

Jon Turney, ed., *Sci-Tech Report: Current Issues in Science and Technology*, Pluto, 1984, Pp. xiii + 386, pb £8.95.

Lord Vansittart, *Roots of the Trouble*, Hutchinson & Co. Ltd., Pp. 32, pb.

Donald Phillip Verene, ed., *Symbol, Myth, and Culture: Essays and Lectures of Ernst Cassirer 1935-1945*, New Haven and London, Yale University Press, 1979, Pp. xii + 304, pb $9.95.

Diane Werneke, *Microelectronics and Office Jobs: The Impact of the Chip on Women's Employment*, Geneva, International Labour Office, Pp. 102, pb £5.45.

Barry Wilkinson, *The Shopfloor Politics of New Technology*, Heinemann Educational Books, 1983, Pp. viii + 120, pb £5.95.

Richard Wollheim and James Hopkins, eds., *Philosophical Essays on Freud*, Cambridge University Press, 1982, Pp. xlv + 314, pb £7.95.

Peter Worsley, *Marx and Marxism*, Chichester, Ellis Horwood and London, Tavistock Publications, 1982, Pp. 126, pb £3.25.

ANTIPODE

A Radical Journal of Geography,
Volume 16, Number 2, 1984

THE FOURTH WORLD
A Geography of Indigenous Struggles

"What defines Fourth World people? They are distinguished by their utilization of the land as a common resource base, their cultural attachment to place (and the unifying force of that attachment), their fundamentally ecological view, their inherently flexible systems of economy and exchange, their adaptiveness to change (when they can control the rate of change), and   dependence on cooperative systems of enterprise, extended kinship systems, and reciprocity. Place, to them, is something much more than a commodity, and it is that attachment to place as other than a commodity which is at the root of the exploitation of Fourth Worlders by others: those who commodify land have found it extraordinarily easy to seize it from those who do not . . . ."
— From the introduction to the issue

American Indians, the Orang Asli of Malaysia, Bedouin, Tuareg, Miskito Indians, and Tribal Development, 64 pp., all in:

Single copies: $5.00. Subscriptions for 1984— special introductory rate of $10.00 (includes Volume 16, No. 3 — *Women and Environment*)

Antipode, P.O. Box 339, West Side Station, Worcester, MA 01602, USA. (Make checks out to *Antipode*.)

NOTES ON CONTRIBUTORS

DAVID ALBURY teaches on the Cultural Studies degree at North East London Polytechnic. He was a founder member of the *Radical Science Journal* and is currently thinking about a book on objectivity and sexuality.

TOM ATHANASIOU is an ecologist, programmer, writer and left-communist, not necessarily in that order.

RICHARD BARBROOK has been involved in the Community Radio Project, which is attempting to set up a radio resource centre in the London Borough of Camden. As a Labour Party member, he is part of *London Labour Briefing*. He teaches politics at the University of Kent at Canterbury, where he is writing a thesis – 'Value, Price and Broadcasting' – on radio as a capitalist labour process.

MICHAEL CHANAN is a film maker and writer. His recent films include *El Salvador – Portrait of a Liberated Zone*, co-directed in 1981 with Peter Chappell, and in 1983 a pair of documentaries for Channel Four Television, *New Cinema of Latin America*. He also co-produced Jorge Denti's *Malvinas, A Story of Betrayals*. His books include *The Dream That Kicks – The Prehistory and Early Years of Cinema in Britain* (Routledge & Kegan Paul, 1980) and a number of monographs published by the BFI, for whom he has also written *The Cuban Image – Cinema and Cultural Politics in Cuba* (1985).

DEEDEE HALLECK produces *Paper Tiger Television*, a weekly series on Manhattan Cable Public Access. For many years she has been involved in directing and producing films, including *Peliculas, Haiti: Bitter Cane*, and *Waiting for the Invasion: US Citizens in Nicaragua* and many more. She has also taught film and served on the board of film-makers' organisations.

URSULA HUWS has been an active trade unionist and feminist, and helped to found Leeds TUCRIC. She is now living precariously as a self-employed researcher and writer in London.

DOUGLAS KELLNER is author of books on Karl Korsch and on Herbert Marcuse, has co-edited a book on expressionism with Stephen Bronner, *Passion and Rebellion: The Expressionist Heritage*, and is co-author of a forthcoming book with Michael Ryan, *Camera Politica: The Politics and Ideology of Contemporary Hollywood Film*. Kellner teaches philosophy at the University of Texas at Austin and is active in radical media work.

LES LEVIDOW is a freelance subversive. He works in the Radical Science Collective, Free Association Books, the National Interest band and other activities undermining civilisation as we know it. He also poisons the minds of our nation's youth at Middlesex Polytechnic.

ARMAND MATTELART is Director of the Inforcom Department at the University of Haute-Bretagne (Rennes II) outside Paris. He founded and co-directs the journal *Communicación y Cultura*.

During 1962–73 he was a university professor in Santiago, and under Allende he worked on mass communications projects. He is author of many publications, including *Transnationals and the Third World* (Bergin & Garvey, 1983) and *International Image Markets* (Comedia, 1984).

COMRADELY PUBLICATIONS AND GROUPS

(Prices are subject to change)

ALTERNATIVE PRESS INDEX
Alternative Press Centre. P.O. Box
7209, Baltimore, MD 21218, USA.

AMPO Japan-Asia Quarterly
Review
P.O. Box 5250, Tokyo International,
Japan. 4 issues p.a. for $16, $24 inst.

ANTIPODE-A Radical Journal of
Geography
P.O. Box 339, West Side Station,
Worcester, MA 01602, USA. 4 issues
for $12 employed, $8 unemployed,
foreign $2 extra.

ARENA-A Marxist Journal of
Criticism and Discussion
P.O. Box 18, North Carlton, Victoria
3054, Australia. 4 issues for A $8,
overseas A $14.

ASSOCIATION OF RADICAL
MIDWIVES
c/o 13 Fremont Street, London E9,
Tel. 986 8939.

BERKELEY JOURNAL OF
SOCIOLOGY
458A Barrows Hall, Dept. of
Sociology, Berkeley, CA 94720, USA.
Subscription $5 individual, $10 inst.

CAHIERS GALILEE
c/o G. Valenduc, 5 rue de la
Resistance, 1490 Court-St-Etienne,
Belgium, special issues on
biotechnology, infotech, 80 FB each.

CASHIERS GERSULP
Univ. de Strasbourg, 67070
Strasbourg, France.

CAPITAL & CLASS-Journal of the
Conference of Socialist Economists
(CSE)
25 Horsell Road, London N5.
Membership rates: £9, low income £6,
overseas £10/£6, for 3 issues p.a.

CINE-TRACTS-A Journal of Film
and Cultural Studies
Institute of Cinema Studies, 4227
Esplanade Ave., Montreal H2W,
Quebec, Canada. 4 issues p.a. for $10,
foreign $12, inst. $20.

COMMENT-Libertarian newsletter

published by Murray Bookchin
P.O. Box 371, Hoboken, NJ 07030,
USA. Send stamped SAE.

COUNTER-INFORMATION
SERVICES (CIS)
9 Poland Street, London W1. The
Nuclear Disaster, 85p; The New
Technology, 95p.

CRIME AND SOCIAL JUSTICE
– A Journal of Radical Criminology
P.O. Box 40601, San Francisco, CA
94140, USA. 2 issues $8, $18 inst.;
foreign $10/$20.

CRITIQUE-A Journal of Soviet
Studies and Socialist Theory
9 Poland St., London W1.

CRITIQUE OF
ANTHROPOLOGY
P.O. Box 178, London WC1 6BU

DEMOCRATIC PALESTINE
(formerly PFLP Bulletin) Box 12144
Damascus, Syria. $15 p.a. for 12
issues.

DIALOGO SOCIAL
Ediciones CCS, Apartado 9A-192,
Panama, R.P.

The GUARDIAN-Independent
Radical Newsweekly
33 West 17th St., New York, NY
10011.

HEAD & HAND-Socialist Review
of Books
CSE Books, 25 Horsell Road, London
N5.

HEALTH/PAC (Policy Advisory
Committee) BULLETIN
17 Murray St., New York, NY 10007.

HISTORY WORKSHOP-A
Journal of Socialist and Feminist
Historians
c/o Routledge & Kegan Paul plc,
Broadway House, Newtown Rd.,
Henley-on-Thames, Oxfordshire RG9
1EN. 2 issues p.a. for £10 ind., £15
inst.

IN THESE TIMES-The
Independent Socialist Newspaper
1509 North Milwaukee Avenue,

Chicago, Illinois 60622, USA. 50
issues for $19 p.a., $35 inst., $32
abroad.
INSURGENT SOCIOLOGIST
Dept. of Sociology, Univ. of Oregon,
Eugene, OR 97403, USA. 4 issues p.a.
for $20 individual, $10 low income,
$20 inst.
INTERNATIONAL JOURNAL OF
HEALTH SERVICES
Baywood Publishing Company, 120
Marine St., Farmingdale NY 11735,
USA. 4 issues for $25 p.a., $20
students, $42 inst.
ISIS–Women's International
Information and Communication
Service
Via Santa Maria dell'Anima 30,
Rome, Italy. 4 issues p.a. for $15, $25
inst. Also available: 'Women in
Development: a resource guide for
organization and action', $12;
'Women and New Technology'.
The JOURNAL OF COMMUNITY
COMMUNICATIONS
Village Design, P.O. Box 996,
Berkeley, CA 94701, USA. $9 for 4
issues, $15 institutions & Foreign.
The LEFT INDEX
551 Lincoln Street, Santa Cruz, CA
95060. 4 issues p.a. for $30 ind., $50
inst.
The LEVELLER
52 Acre Lane, London SW2. £7 p.a.,
£15.00 inst.
LITERATURE TEACHING
POLITICS
c/o Andrew Belsey, Dept. of
Philosophy, University College,
Cardiff CF1 1XL.
MEDICINE IN SOCIETY–
Quarterly Socialist Journal of Health
Studies.
16 St. John Street, London EC1. £6
p.a. individual, £7 inst., £9 overseas.
MIDNIGHT NOTES
Box 204, Jamaica Plain, MA 02130. 3
issues for $4. Special issues on the
anti-nuclear movement, the work/
energy crisis, space notes, the
computer state, political lemmings.
Back issues $2, or £1.50 from Radical
Science.

MODERNE ZEITEN (Socialist
Monthly)
Am Taubenfelde 30, 3000 Hanover 1,
W. Germany. 10 issues p.a. for DM
60.
MOTHER JONES–A Magazine
For The Rest of Us.
625 Third Street, San Francisco, CA
94107, USA. 10 issues p.a. for $22, $22
overseas.
MONTHLY REVIEW–An
Independent Socialist Magazine
62 West 14th St., New York, NY
10011, USA. 10 issues for $22
individual, $33 institutional p.a., $11
students, $18/$13 foreign.
MULTINATIONAL MONITOR
1346 Connecticut Ave., NW, Room
411, Washington D.C. 20036. 12 issues
p.a. for $18 individual, $25 non-profit
institutions, $35 business institutions,
foreign – add $8 air-mail.
NATURKAMPEN
c/o Politisk Revy, St. Pederstraede
28B, Copenhagen, Denmark.
NEW GERMAN CRITIQUE– An
Interdisciplinary Journal of German
Studies
German Dept., Box 413, Univ. of
Milwaukee, WI 53201, USA. 3 issues
p.a. for $11 individual, $22 inst.,
foreign $1 extra.
OPEN ROAD–Anarcha-Feminist
Edition
Box 6135, Station G, Vancouver, B.C.,
Canada. Send 1 hour's pay for a sub.
OXFORD LITERARY REVIEW–A
Post-structuralist Journal
2 Marlborough Road, Oxford OX1
4LP, U.K. 2 issues p.a. for £5/$9, inst.
£6/$16.
PACIFIC RESEARCH–Global
Electronics Information Newsletter
Pacific Studies Center, 222B View
Street, Mountain View, CA 94041,
USA. 4 issues p.a. for $5, $7, foreign,
$11 inst. 'Changing Role of S.E.
Asian Women', $2; 'Delicate Bonds:
The Global Semiconductor Industry',
$2.
PANDORE–Problems of Science,
Technology and Society
c/o Denise de Pouvorville, 2 rue

Conté, 75141 Paris, France.
PHILOSOPHY & SOCIAL
ACTION
M-120 Greater Kailash-1, New Delhi-
110 048, India. 4 issues p.a. for $15
ind., $35 inst.
POLITICS OF HEALTH
Newsletter
POHG, c/o BSSRS, Poland Street,
London W1. Send £2 + six sae's.
PRAXIS-A Journal of Radical
Perspectives on the Arts.
Dickson Arts Center, UCLA, Los
Angeles, CA 90024. 2 issues for $8; or
from Pluto Press, £5.
PROCESSED WORLD-The
Magazine With A Bad Attitude
55 Sutter Street, no. 829; San
Francisco, CA 94101. 4 issues for $10
ind., $15 inst. & Overseas.
PSYCHOLOGY & SOCIAL
THEORY
East Hill Branch, Box 2740, Ithaca,
NY 14850. 2 issues p.a. for $10 ind.,
$20 inst.
RACE & CLASS-A Journal for
Black and Third World Liberation
Institute of Race Relations, 247
Pentonville Road, London N1. 4
issues p.a. for £8/$16 individual, £12/
$30 inst.
RACE TODAY-Voice of the Black
Community in Britain
165 Railton Road, London SE24.
£6 ind., £14 inst.
RADICAL AMERICA
38 Union Square, Somerville, MA
02143, USA. 6 issues p.a. for $15
individual, $8 unemployed, foreign $3
extra; double for institutions.
RADICAL BOOKSELLER
265 Seven Sisters Road, London N4.
10 issues p.a. for £10 individual, £15
others.
RADICAL COMMUNITY
MEDICINE
c/o Alex Scott-Samuel, 5 Lyndon
Drive, Liverpool L18 6HP, U.K. 4
issues p.a. for £6, £8 foreign (£11
airmail).
RADICAL HISTORY REVIEW
Mid-Atlantic Radical Historians'
Organization (MARHO), John Jay

College, 445 West 59th St., New York,
NY 10019, USA. 3 issues p.a. for $14
ind., $10 unemployed, $30 inst., plus
$4 extra abroad.
RADICAL PHILOSOPHY
c/o Ian Craib, Dept. Sociology, Univ.
of Essex, Colchester CO4 3SQ, U.K.
£3.25 for 3 issues p.a., £5 overseas.
RADICAL STATISTICS-Bulletin
of BSSRS Radical Statistics Group
9 Poland St., London W1. 3 issues
p.a. for £3, £5 inst., £1.50 for unwaged.
RED LETTERS-Communist Party
Literature Journal
16 St. John Street, London EC1.
REVIEW OF AFRICAN
POLITICAL ECONOMY
341 Glossop Road, Sheffield S10
2HP, UK. 3 issues p.a. for £6 in UK
& Africa, $13 elsewhere. No. 22 on
'Ideology, Class and Development',
£2.
REVIEW OF RADICAL
POLITICAL ECONOMICS (URPE)
155 W. 23rd St., 12th fl. New York,
NY 10011, USA. $4.50 per copy.
REVOLUON-Tijdschrift Over
Technologie, Natuurwetenschappen
en Kapitaal.
Postbus 1328, 6501 Nijmegen,
Holland. 4 issues for fl7.50 p.a.
REVOLUTIONARY SOCIALISM-
Big Flame Magazine
217 Wavertree Road, Liverpool 7.
The RIPENING OF TIME-
Theoretical Journal
P.O. Box 1103, 29 Mountjoy Square,
Dublin 1, Ireland.
SCHOOLING & CULTURE
ILEA Cockpit Arts Workshop,
Gateforth Street, London NW8. 3
issues p.a. for £5., £9 overseas.
SCIENCE & SOCIETY
Room 4331 John Jay College, CUNY,
445 West 59th St., New York, NY
10019, USA. 4 issues p.a. for $12,
foreign $19; $30 inst.
SCIENCE-FICTION STUDIES
Prof. Philmus, English Dept.
Concordia University, 7141
Sherbrooke St. West, Montreal,
Quebec, Canada H4B 1R6. 3 issues
p.a. for $12 individual/$19 inst., $10/

$16.50 in USA.

SCIENCE FOR PEOPLE-
Magazine of BSSRS
9 Poland St., London W1. 4 issues
p.a. for £4 individual, £10 inst. 10%
extra for foreign currency.

SCIENCE FOR THE PEOPLE-
Magazine of SESPA
897 Main Street, Cambridge, MA
02139, USA. 6 issues p.a. for $15, $24
inst. overseas, add $13 (airmail). Nov/
Dec 1981 issue on 'Wrestling with
Automation', $1.50. 15th anniversary
issue, $2.

SCIENCE FOR THE VILLAGES
c/o Anand Kumar, Magan
Sangrahalaya, 442001 Wardha
Maharashlia, India.

SE-SCIENZA ESPERIENZA
Via Valtellina 20, 20159 Milano, Italy.
(This monthly magazine is a sequel
to *Sapere*.)

SIGNS-Journal of Women in
Culture and Society
University of Chicago Press, 5801
Ellis Avenue, Chicago, Illinois 60637,
USA. 4 issues p.a. for $15., single
copy $4.

SOCIALISM AND EDUCATION-
Journal of the Socialist Education
Association, 14 Branscombe St.,
London SE13 7AY. 3 issues for £1.50
p.a.; membership £4.

SOCIALIST HEALTH REVIEW
19 June Blossom Society, 60A Pali
Road, Bandra (West), Bombay 400
050, India. 4 issues p.a. for $20.

SYGHRONA THEMATA
c/o Giorgos Goulakos, Valaoritou 12,
Athens 134, Greece.

TECHNOLOGY & CULTURE
University of Chicago Press, 5801

Ellis Avenue, Chicago, Illinois 60637,
USA.

TELOS-A Quarterly Journal of
Radical Thought
Box 3111, St. Louis, MO 63130 USA.
$22 for 4 issues p.a., $50 institutions,
overseas, add 10%, cheques in US$
only.

TERMINAL 19/84-Centre
d'Information et d'Initiative sur
l'Informatisation
C.I.I.I., 1 Rue Keller, 75011 Paris,
France.

TESTI E CONTESTI-Quaderni di
Scienze, Storia e Societa.
CLUP, Piazza Leonardo da Vinci 32,
Milano, Italy. 3 issues for Lit. 15,000,
foreign 20,000.

UNDERCURRENTS
27a Clerkenwell Close, London EC1.
10 issues p.a. for £7 individual, £9
inst.

UTUSAN KONSUMER
Consumers Association Penang, No.
27 Kelawei Road, Pulau Pinang,
Malaysia.

WECHSELWIRKUNG-
Technik/Naturwissenschaft/
Gesellschaft
Gneisenaustr. 2, 1000
Berlin 61, W. Germany. 4 issues for
20 Dm.

**WETENSCHAP EN
SAMENLEVING VWO**
Stadhouderslaan 91, 3583 JG Utrecht,
Holland. 10 issues for f35.

WIRE (Women's International
Resource Exchange)
2700 Broadway, New York, NY 10025,
USA. New free catalog includes
reports on health care and Third
World issues.

BACK ISSUES OF Radical Science Journal
STILL AVAILABLE

RSJ 5
BOB YOUNG: Science *is* Social Relations/PATRICK PARRINDER: Science
and Social Consciousness in SF/DAVID TRIESMAN: The Institute of
Psychiatry Sackings

RSJ 6/7 The Labour Process
LES LEVIDOW: A Marxist Critique of the IQ Debate/MIKE BARNETT:
Technology and the Labour Process/BOB YOUNG: Getting Started on
Lysenkoism/RSJ SUBGROUP: Marxism, Feminism and Psychoanalysis/
LES LEVIDOW: Grunwick as Technology and Class Struggle

RSJ 8
DAVID DICKSON: Science and Political Hegemony in the 17th Century/
WENDY HOLLWAY: Ideology and Medical Abortion/PHILIP BOYS:
Detente, Genetics, and Social Theory

RSJ 9 Medicine
KARL FIGLIO: Sinister Medicine?/GIANNA POMATA: Seveso – Safety in
Numbers?/LES LEVIDOW: Three Mile Island/Critical Bibliography on
Medicine

RSJ 10 Third World
DAVID DICKSON: Science and Technology, North and South:
Multinational Management for Underdevelopment/RAPHAEL
KAPLINSKY: Microelectronics and the Third World/LES LEVIDOW:
Notes on Development/BRIAN MARTIN: The Goal of Self-Managed
Science

RSJ 11
RSJ COLLECTIVE: Science, Technology, Medicine and the Socialist
Movement/JONATHAN REE: The Anti-Althusser Bandwagon/PAM LINN:
Designer or Drone?/MAUREEN McNEIL: Braverman Revisited

RSJ 12 Medicalisation
INTRODUCTION: Unnatural Childbirth?/JANET JENNINGS: Who
Controls Childbirth?/SHELLEY DAY: Is Obstetric Technology
Depressing?/EVAN STARK: What is Medicine?

RSJ 13 Scientism in the Left
STEVE SMITH: Taylorism Rules OK? Bolshevism, Taylorism and the
Technical Intelligentsia/LES LEVIDOW: We Won't Be Fooled Again?
Economic Planning and Left Strategies/DOUG KELLNER: Science and
Method in Marx's Capital/JOE CROCKER: Sociobiology: The Capitalist
Synthesis/TIM PUTNAM: Proletarian Science?

RSJ 14 No Clear Reason: Nuclear Power Politics
INTRODUCTION: No Clear Reason/MIDNIGHT NOTES COLLECTIVE:
'Exterminism' or Class Struggle?/JAMES WOOD: Why Cruise and
Pershing?/DAVE ROSENFELD: Don't Just Reduce Risk – Transform It!/
LES LEVIDOW and BOB YOUNG: Exhibiting Nuclear Power: The Science
Museum Cover-Up/MARTIN SPENCE: Exporting the 'Peaceful Atom'/
DHIRENDRA SHARMA: India's Nuclear Estate: An Interview/T.V.
SATHYAMURTHY: India's Post-Colonial Nuclear Estate/STEPHEN
ROBINSON: Nuclear States of Terror
No. 14 Price: £5 individual, £6 institutional.

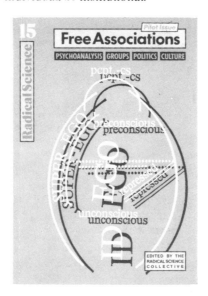

RSJ 15 Free Associations: Psychoanalysis, Groups, Politics, Culture
Editorial/ROBERT M. YOUNG: No Easy Answers/RUSSELL JACOBY:
Remembering 'Social Amnesia'/JANE TEMPERLEY: Our Own Worst
Enemies: Unconscious Factors in Female Disadvantage/DAVID INGLEBY:
The Ambivalence of Psychoanalysis/MARGOT WADDELL: The Long
Weekend/BARRY RICHARDS: Civil Defence and Psychic Defence/
MICHAEL RUSTIN: Psychoanalysis and Social Justice/KARL FIGLIO:
Freud's Exegesis of the Soul/STEPHEN ROBINSON: The Art of the
Possible/JOEL KOVEL: On Being a Marxist Psychoanalyst (and a Psy-
choanalytic Marxist)
No. 15 Price: £5.50 individual.

Back Issue Price: £3 individual, £5 institutional.
If ordering direct with payment in foreign currency, add equivalent of
60p to cover bank charges and use current exchange rates.
Radical Science Journal, 26 Freegrove Road, London N7 9RQ

RADICAL SCIENCE provides a forum for extended analyses of the ideology and practice of science, technology and medicine from a radical political perspective. Most contributors have attempted to re-examine past Marxist views and to develop a Marxist critique of the role of scientism in the Left.

We welcome suggestions for thematic numbers emphasising particular topics around the critique of power exercised through expertise. We would like especially to develop a positive programme for the role of oppositional knowledge.

Radical Science Collective

This serial is edited and produced by a collective whose members are Gavin Browning, Joe Crocker, Karl Figlio, Mike Hales, Chris Knee, Les Levidow, Pam Linn, Maureen McNeil, Barry Richards, Tony Solomonides, Margot Waddell and Bob Young.

Overseas Contacts

ITALY: Gianna Pomata, Via Bertiera 7/2, Bologna.
FRANCE: John Stewart, 27 rue de Montreuil, Paris 75011. Tel. 356.10.71.
David Dickson, Le Billehau, St Aubin, 91190 Gif-su-yvette.
AUSTRALIA: Brian Martin, Maths. Faculties, ANU, PO Box 4, Canberra ACT 2600 Tel. (062) 494445, home tel. (062) 485426

Editorial Contributions

Ideally, articles should be less than 10,000 words and typed double-spaced. A number of copies would help: it is our policy that all articles should be read by as many members of the collective as possible. This usually takes some time so please bear with us – but remind us when your patience runs out.

Subscriptions to RADICAL SCIENCE

The subscription for three numbers is £14.00 post paid, libraries and institutions £18.00. Numbers appear at irregular intervals, so the subscription is not annual: it covers three consecutive numbers. For details of back numbers see inside rear cover. Those who support us in our project are invited to add a donation to their subscription. Subscription to *Free Associations* (published quarterly): £20/$25 per annum for individuals; £35/$45 for institutions. Single copies: £5.50/$6.50. Please add the equivalent of £0.60 to foreign cheques to cover bank charges involved. Subscriptions, donations, enquiries and articles should be sent to:

Free Association Books, 26 Freegrove Road, London N7 9RQ. Tel. (01) 609 5646.

Distribution

UK: Turnaround, 25 Horsell Road, London N5. Tel. (01) 609 7836.
S&N, 48a Hamilton Place, Edinburgh EH3 5AX. Tel. (031) 225 4590.
18 Granby Row, Manchester M1 3GE. Tel. (061) 228 3903.
USA: B.deBoer, 113 East Center Street, Nutley, NJ 07119. Tel. (201) 667 9300.
Carrier Pigeon, 40 Plympton St., Boston, MA 02118. Tel. (617) 542 5679.
CANADA: DEC, 427 Bloor St West, Toronto, Ontario M5S 1X7. Tel. (416) 964 6560.
AUSTRALIA: Astam Books, 250 Abercrombie Street, Chippendale, NSW 2008. Tel. Sydney 698 4080.

Production

Typeset by Folio Photosetting, Bristol.
Printed in Great Britain by SRP Ltd., Exeter

Copyright

Cover Design

Carlos Sapochnik, 6 Ridge Road, London N8. Tel (01) 341 9147.